Studies in Sociology

The Development of Modern Sociology

Its Nature and Growth in the United States

By ROSCOE C. HINKLE, JR.
And GISELA J. HINKLE
Ohio State University

RANDOM HOUSE
New York

301
H59d

LIBRARY OF CONGRESS CATALOG CARD NUMBER: 54-11807
MANUFACTURED IN THE UNITED STATES OF AMERICA

Editor's Foreword

Sociology enjoys an unequalled popularity in this country and is often called an "American science." But this designation is misleading in several respects, the most important of which, certainly, is the canon of universality that governs—or should govern—all science. Moreover, the "American" label obscures sociology's European origins and the long-standing but intermittent influence of numerous non-American scholars. If the works of Comte and Spencer carried heavy weight among the American Fathers of sociology, so today the theories of Durkheim, Pareto, Max Weber, and, increasingly, Freud, to name outstandingly influential figures, are cited in current texts, employed in research, and sounded in the classroom.

Yet the international status of sociology is only partial. From the beginning, sociology in the United States—like our philosophy and political science and folkthought—has been largely a product of native conditions. The role of changing American culture and social structure in the development of modern sociology is itself an important sociological lesson. Thus changing emphases in the conception of the nature of the subject and of its appropriate tasks, in concrete investigatory problems, and even in method reflect, directly and indirectly, such major features of the American historical experience as the frontier and its closure, urbanization and industrialization, large-scale immigration, political democracy and anti-democratic developments, ever-extending public education, deeply rooted Christian doctrine, growing bureaucratization in more and more areas, and, not least, two World Wars and the Great Depression.

Although the authors, Roscoe and Gisela Hinkle, disclaim that this study is a "sociology of sociology," they bring out the several ways in which these various circumstances have helped to shape sociological thought and practice. Their analysis of the growth and uneven course of American sociology during three discernible stages—the 19th and early 20th century period of the pioneers, the years of empirical preoccupation in the 1920s and early 1930s, and the subsequent partial convergence of theory and research and application—also indicates the significant influence of the theories of diverse European scholars. In these respects, the Hinkles make an important contribution to the history of sociology.

But the authors do not stop at this point. Their study is much more than a running account of a large part of the sociological story: it is an informed and unique interpretation of the "American" science. They find a persistent point of view in American sociology, from which to be sure several contributors have departed, but which marks the writings of, say,

Lester F. Ward in the initial period and those of such contrasting individuals as Robert M. MacIver and Talcott Parsons today. The Hinkles refer to this point of view as *voluntaristic nominalism*, itself an orientation consistent with the social and cultural conditions of American life. (Indeed, a strong case can be made that "voluntaristic nominalism" characterizes a sizeable portion of American intellectual production in general.) This concept enhances the analysis all along and increases, I believe, the validity of treating within a single framework—called "'social action" theory by the Hinkles; it might be termed *inter*action theory—the views of Florian Znaniecki, MacIver, Howard Becker, and Parsons.

Some readers may take issue with the Hinkles' interpretation here and there. (For example, I disagree with their use of "individualism" at certain points.) But few instructors will fail to find this study a valuable teaching instrument. It provides both the college and general student a brief but unusually thorough and clearly presented account of the development of sociology in the United States. For classroom use, the study's brevity permits it to be assigned in combination with other readings, especially with original sources that all too frequently are neglected. The succinct portrayals of the views of a large number of leading sociologists constitute a highly useful addition to the literature for student and teacher alike. Finally, *The Development of Modern Sociology* is a convenient point of departure for the instructor who wishes, as most of us do, to develop his own emphasis. For varying interpretations of the accomplishments—and failures—of our science are enabled by the judicious representativeness with which the Hinkles have selected their materials and the objectivity of their presentation.

CHARLES H. PAGE

Preface

IIIIIIIIIIIIIIIIIIIIIIIIIIIIIIIIIIIIIIIIIIIIIIIIIIIIIIIIIIIIIIIIIIIIIIIIIIIIIIIIIIIIIIIIIIIIIIIIIIIIIIIIIIIIIIIIIIIIIIIIIIIIIIIIIIIIIIIIIIIIIIIIIIIIIIIIIIIIIIIIIIIIIIIIII

The Development of Modern Sociology is written to assist the student in attaining a more integrated understanding of contemporary American sociology. The present specialization of subfields, techniques, and orientations, which may often seem confusingly diverse, becomes meaningful when the discipline's continuities with, and differences from, the past are outlined. The authors have therefore attempted to present a panoramic view of the major changes and identifying landmarks of American sociology over the last fifty years.

This presentation is based on the available, published data of what sociologists are doing and have done. Adoption of one viewpoint to define the field is thus intentionally avoided. A specific definition requires selective inclusion of data which would confuse the student as well as obstruct the goal of the authors. Accordingly, the point of departure is the on-going activities of sociologists in their professional role as social scientists. The authors are not concerned with the question of which point of view *should* be preferred *to advance* the field *scientifically*.

Since the American student is most frequently exposed to the field as it has been developed and interpreted in this country, the inquiry has concentrated its attention on American sociology. Although it is a product of both European and native intellectual influences, the discipline is uniquely American in organization and development. Foreign contributions are noted only as they have had demonstrable and significant impact on the American scene.

Understanding the peculiarly American character of modern sociology requires that the reader become familiar with some of the continuities throughout the early, intermediate, and modern periods of the discipline. The divisions of 1905–1918, 1918–1935, 1935–1954 are based on certain unique social events and changes in the development of sociology. Nevertheless, there are recurrences within the problems studied, methods used, and assumptions made about the nature of scientific methodology, the nature of human nature, and the nature of society. Their persistence has given the field its continuity and interrelatedness.

Perhaps the outstandingly persistent feature of American sociology is its *voluntaristic nominalism*. This term describes the assumption that the structure of all social groups is the consequence of the aggregate of its separate, component individuals and that social phenomena ultimately derive from the motivations of these knowing, feeling, and willing individuals.

The study also attempts to show that the intellectual content of sociology is related to and dependent on its social context—the organization of professional sociologists, broader intellectual currents, and the larger social and cultural setting. While it does not pretend to be a sociology of sociology, it does try to make the student aware that the nature of sociology is not merely the result of a self-contained development, unaffected by trends outside the discipline itself.

Finally, contributions of principal figures in sociology are related to the dominant currents in the field. Reference is made to leading personalities only as they have been involved in the fundamental polemics about the core-problems, the primary methods, and the basic assumptions pervading sociology during the last fifty years. Consequently, there is no attempt to present the entire range of intellectual work of any one of these major sociologists.

This preoccupation with major trends has obviously necessitated omissions. For instance, the incorporation and acceptance of the concept of culture from anthropology has not been explained. Nor has any effort been made to indicate the developments within such subfields as criminology, family life, social stratification, industrial sociology, public opinion, etc. Such descriptions are more appropriately the province of other studies.

The authors are both greatly indebted to Charles H. Page, editor of the Random House Studies in Sociology. Not only has he made innumerable constructive suggestions about style and content, but from the very beginning he has shown untiring patience.

ROSCOE C. HINKLE, JR.
GISELA J. HINKLE

Contents

chapter one

The Foundation of American Sociology
(1905–1918)

To understand contemporary American sociology is to see its continuity with the past. In spite of apparent differences between the discipline's earlier and modern phases, current sociology has been shaped by certain characteristics of the formative era. Emerging in a social setting of rapid urbanization and industrialization after the Civil War, the field concerned itself with social problems. In studying these problems early sociologists employed the assumptions of natural law, progress, meliorism, and individualism. Yet their interests were unspecialized. In addition to the generality of interests, the small number of sociologists and members of the American Sociological Society contributed to the early undifferentiated state of sociology. Although the men, who had come out of very diverse intellectual backgrounds, knew one another personally, they carried on their research as individuals rather than as members of research teams.

Although its earlier and contemporary phases may thus seem vastly different, the discipline shows certain persistent intellectual characteristics. However halting and unsuccessful early sociologists' attempt to establish a scientific discipline may seem today, modern sociologists are continuing this same endeavor. They are still preoccupied with the formulation of laws of human behavior, though they may not agree with their earlier colleagues that these laws automatically reveal themselves as part of a natural order. As in the past, the study of society is largely undertaken from the perspective of individualism. Explaining and predicting social change remains a basic, if not the fundamental, concern of sociology. Social problems which were associated with the earlier study of change are the foundation for the specific fields today. Finally, the usefulness of sociological knowledge continues to be invoked—either implicitly or explicitly—to justify sociological activities, though the earlier commitments to progress and reform have been largely abandoned. Understanding these persistencies requires a study of the various aspects of early American sociology.

The Social Setting of Early Sociology

Whether its establishment is dated from the founding of the American Sociological Society in 1905, from the increasing inclusion of courses bearing the name in academic institutions in the 1890s, or from the appearance of publications dealing with the subject in the 1880s, American sociology emerged in a social context in which the city and the factory were the principal monuments of change. Few of the early sociologists would have seriously questioned the propriety of defining as progress the accumulating artifacts of living and the increasing mastery over nature wrought by the application of science to technology in the nascent urban-industrial society. The welding of the nation into one economic unit with a mass market for mass production and mass consumption, supported by large-scale agriculture and founded on the exploitation of the country's raw materials, elaboration of technology, accumulation of capital for investment, and expansion of railroads, produced the implements of physical comfort. More than others, the urbanite's mode of life was affected by this efflorescence of gadgetry. By the early 1900s he had heard of the airplane, seen an automobile, and—more than likely—had direct experience with the elevated and the subway, the incandescent light bulb, the telephone, the multicelled department store, and the skyscraper. Census figures confirm the migration to the city.

But many early American sociologists who were tutored in the ideals of a frontier social democracy and the personalized intimacy of agrarian society were reluctant to regard the associated economic and social transformations as moral progress. The sphere of small business was more narrowly confined as the old-time individual entrepreneur, who worked shoulder to shoulder with his help, was replaced by the corporation with its anonymity and more formal management corps. The rise of industrial and financial giants was accompanied by a magnification of status differences and a consolidation of political and economic control. Many of these men flaunted their amassed wealth in the form of conspicuous leisure and consumption. Personifying the forces of change, they were often the targets of the discontent engendered by both rural and urban impoverishment. From the farmers' viewpoint, these men had engineered the price decline, subjected them to usurious rates of interest on their mortgages, squeezed them by high freight rates, and fleeced them by fraudulent bond issues. They were often seen as the ogres behind the squalor and poverty of the urban slums. Their machinations were blamed for the downward gyrations of the business cycle which endangered the worker's job, for the inundation of immigrant workers who depressed wages or threatened the worker's job, and for the adoption of a more efficient technology which caused the obsolescence of skills.

These social dislocations associated with industrialization and urbanization generated public protest and social reform movements. The Grangers (or the Patrons of Husbandry), the Knights of Labor, and the later American Federation of Labor became specialized organizations for the occupational interests of the farmer and worker; the Greenback, Single-Tax, Populist, and Progressive political movements developed; from the Protestant churches came the Social Gospel Movement as a vehicle for reform; and through the medium of the emerging popular literature of the period the muckrakers exposed economic, political, and social injustices. Among those who hoped to employ science in the amelioration of social evils were the sociologists.

Evidence from at least four sources supports the view that sociology emerged largely as a response to the industrialization and urbanization of the post-Civil War era. First, the characteristic social backgrounds of those men whose careers figured prominently in the ascendancy of sociology testify to this fact. The vast majority of eminent sociologists prior to 1920 came from rural and religious environments. Of the nineteen presidents of the American Sociological Society who had been born prior to 1880, who had completed their graduate studies before 1910, and who had achieved some prominence before 1920, not one had experienced a typically urban childhood.[1] Although some of these sociologists can hardly be identified with an endorsement of the ideology and practices of conventional, institutionalized religion of their era, they were almost without exception fundamentally concerned with ethical issues. This concern can be understood when it is realized that these men grew to maturity at a time when the religious and ethical traditions of Protestantism still dominated the nation. Often their reformism was a secular version of the Christian concern with salvation and redemption and was a direct outgrowth of religious antecedents in their personal lives. Lester F. Ward's maternal grandfather and Franklin H. Giddings' and William I. Thomas' fathers had been ministers; William G. Sumner, Albion W. Small, George E. Vincent, Edward C. Hayes, James P. Lichtenberger, Ulysses G. Weatherly, and John L. Gillin had themselves had earlier ministerial careers. This recurrent combination of rural background with inculcation of religious ideals was an important part of the experiential framework within which so many early sociologists interpreted and evaluated the conditions and problems of urban, industrial life.

Second, the academic setting within which sociology achieved respectability was of such nature and so located as to be acutely sensitive to effects of urbanization. Sociology courses were introduced before 1905 in such Eastern institutions as Brown, Clark, Columbia, Dartmouth, Pennsylvania, and Yale. Nevertheless, the Midwestern intellectual climate during the post-Civil War educational expansion seems to have been more favorable to early sociology. This circumstance may in part be due to the fact that, unlike the Eastern private schools, the publicly supported state institutions of the Middle West were less encumbered by precedent and tradition in their curricula. The Department of Sociology at the University of Chicago, which was established in 1893 under the chairmanship of Albion W. Small, also profited from this advantage.

Similarly noteworthy is the primary association of the leadership of the new social science with the Midwest. Of the nineteen presidents referred to previously, only Sumner, Giddings, Dealey, and Hankins did not come from or hold academic posts in the Midwest. Ross, Vincent, Cooley, Weatherly, Park, Gillin, and Gillette both grew up and spent their mature academic lives in the area. Small, Howard, Blackmar, Hayes, and Ellwood were best known through their affiliation with Midwestern institutions. Accordingly, twelve major sociologists attained their academic distinction in that region.

The role of the Midwest in the emergence of sociology takes on added significance when its distinctive part in the expansion of urbanism and industrialism during this same period is noted. This region was a kind of frontier where the precipitate social modifications were strongly felt and where reformist arguments were frequently voiced and widely approved.

A third indication of the importance of urbanization and industrialization in the emergence of sociology is provided by the fact that the professional organization of sociologists is a lineal descendant of a general intellectual movement committed to betterment of urban social conditions. From the 1840s to the 1890s, this Social Science Movement, as it was called, passed through several phases: the Associationist, early Comtean, early Systematic, post-Associationist, Nationalist (or Carey Economic) School, Neo-Classical (Economic) School, and that of the American Social Science Association.[2] The last phase derives its name from an organization which was founded in 1865 and which was progenitor of the various specific social science societies. In 1884 the American Economic Association was organized, and its direct offspring, the American Sociological Society, was founded in 1905. Throughout all of its phases, the Social Science Movement was concerned with science and social reform. Even in those instances when science seemed to become an exclusive preoccupation, it was justified as a means to social reform of the conditions accompanying urbanization and industrialization.

A fourth source of evidence relating early sociology to a context of industrial urbanization is provided by the nature of the content of the social science and early sociology college and university courses of the 1890s. At the time that the general social science courses were being transformed into sociology courses (1885–1895), they were predominantly oriented to social problems.[3] Both the courses in social science and in early sociology thus directed their interest to the conditions or issues associated with the urban poor: pauperism, charity, scientific philanthropy, private and public relief, unemployment, migratory labor, child labor, women wage-earners, the labor movement, dependent children, insanity, illness, crime, juvenile delinquency, family instability, temperance, immigration, and race relations.

The Influence of Comte and Spencer

Courses in early American sociology thus reflect the sensitivity of American sociologists to the social changes transpiring in the social setting in which they lived. However, the intellectual framework within which these urban problems were approached was largely shaped by European influences. There was scarcely an American sociologist of this early period who had not read the works of Auguste Comte and Herbert Spencer, two intellectuals who had themselves witnessed the impact of urbanization in France and England respectively.

Auguste Comte (1798–1857) is often called the father of sociology because he presented the first comprehensive, abstract model for the scientific study of society by a discipline which he named *sociology*. He insisted that inquiry into social phenomena becomes scientific by following the uniform course of progressive intellectual development of knowledge. Each of the other, prior fields in the hierarchy of science—first astronomy, next physics, then chemistry, and finally biology—has passed through three general stages of knowledge. In the initial or theological stage supernatural beings are invoked as final causes; imaginary entities are used as explanations in the second or metaphysical stage; and with the advent of the third or positive stage, natural and invariable laws explain structure and change.

Comte was concerned because sociology, which stands at the top of his hierarchy of sciences, had not made the final transition from the metaphysical to the positive level. Believing that the type of knowledge determines the state of social organization, Comte maintained that the attainment of social progress awaits the formulation of universal social laws. Accordingly, he devoted himself to prescribing how to derive the laws of society by using the methods uniformly available to all sciences: observation, experiment, and comparison. Sociology should make particular use of the comparative method and its derivative, the historical method, for they are both adapted from comparison in biology, the science on which sociology is most dependent.

Because every science is generally indebted to the one immediately preceding it in the hierarchy, sociology's organization as a scientific discipline is modeled after biology's. The study of social life is a part of the larger study of life. Just as society is viewed as an organism, so social structure and change are studied like anatomy and physiology. The laws of social statics or coexistence thus state that the parts of society at any one moment in time are as naturally and harmoniously ordered and as mutually interdependent as the parts of an organism. The laws of social dynamics or succession, though they are less immediately related to biology, stipulate that society moves gradually, continuously, inevitably through a series of stages of progressive development. Social progress is a consequence of an improvement in knowledge which accompanies the constant accumulation of experience by successive generations. Nevertheless, progress as Comte conceived it has a biological basis in human nature. On the one hand, there is an instinct urging man to develop his abilities as far as circumstances permit. On the other, improvements in acquired characteristics become incorporated in human nature, are subsequently transmitted through heredity according to Lamarck's thesis, and are ultimately reflected in the advancement of intellect and morals.

But whether society is studied from the perspective of structural or dynamic laws, it must be investigated as an interrelated, organic whole. To divide society into different parts, each studied by a separate discipline, destroys the essential character of its unity and coherence. Thus, Comte's sociology is a basic and synthetic social science embracing the whole of social life.

However, American sociologists were more immediately indebted for their ideas concerning social structure and social change to the monumental work of the English evolutionist, Herbert Spencer (1820–1903). In spite of his personal protest against comparisons with Comte by American sociologists, Spencer was a positivist, convinced that the method of science if applied to the study of society could yield fruitful solutions for man's social maladjustments and could increase man's control over nature.

Spencer sought to explain man's social existence as an extension of more general laws covering all phenomena. He viewed phenomena as fundamentally matter in motion which falls into one of three realms: the inorganic, the organic, and the superorganic. Each realm possesses its respective laws of evolution: the physical, biological, and social. Since Spencer defined society in terms of its constituent individuals and since these are an organic species, the laws of the superorganic realm are derivations of the biological laws of evolution—the struggle for existence and the survival of the fittest. These latter laws, however, are consistent with the physical laws of evolution which are based on the principle of the conservation of energy or the "persistence of force."

In explaining social evolution Spencer used the organic analogy earlier employed by Comte. However, their usages stand in distinct contrast. Comte conceived society as an organic whole which develops historically and is, therefore, different from and greater than the sum of the individuals present within it at any one time. Although Spencer agreed that human society resembles a plant or animal organism, he noted certain differences emphasizing the role of the individual. First, the individuals who are the organs of society are physically free and spatially separate while the parts of an organism are in close contact within a concrete unified whole. Second, social consciousness is diffuse and has no existence apart from the separate consciousness of the component individuals. In contrast, consciousness in plants and animals is centralized and localized in a specific part of the organism. Third, human society exists for the benefit of its individual members, whereas the units of the plant and animal organism exist for the good of the whole. For Spencer, society is a whole only as an aggregate of parts, a kind of additive sum of its constituent individuals.

Following Malthus, he viewed the pressure of subsistence upon population as the basic cause of the progress of mankind since survival is possible only for those with skill, intelligence, self-control, and power to adapt to technological innovation. From generation to generation this biologically-conceived notion of adaptation through the survival of the fittest continues, producing material progress, selecting the best intellects, and augmenting the intellectual powers of the race. Adhering to Lamarck's theory of the inheritance of acquired characteristics, both mental and physical, Spencer could readily envision cumulative social betterment through improved individual quality.

Since evil is a result of the nonadaptation of biological constitution to environmental conditions, evil tends to disappear and moral progress to continue as man improves his methods of meeting the exigencies of life. Ultimately, unfitness will destroy itself as the breach widens between the constitution of the organism and the conditions which it must meet. For this reason, Spencer categorically opposed state interference in the natural growth of society. Aiding the poor and dependent merely means survival of the unfit in society and a weakening of the strength of the group. However, this defense of laissez-faire individualism endeared Spencer more to the industrial magnates of the late nineteenth century in America than it did to most American sociologists.

Within the course of superorganic or social evolution, Spencer argued, this process of individual adaptation accounts for the transformation of society from a militant to an industrial type of social structure. The struggle for existence was formerly indispensable to social evolution, for it consolidated social groups into larger ones and evoked social cooperation. But the very process of consolidation widens the areas in which internal peace and the practice of the industrial arts become habitual. Unlike the older form which bristled with weapons, trained people for warfare, relied upon a despotic state, and submerged the individual in a vast amount of forced cooperation, the industrial society is pacific, respectful of the individual, more heterogeneous and plastic, and more inclined to abandon economic autonomy in favor of international, industrial cooperation. Natural selection develops a type of character congenial to the values of life, liberty, and property. And as human nature is modified by these changed conditions of existence, it will move increasingly from egoism to altruism.

Although Spencer tried vigorously to dissociate himself from Comte, he was often regarded as the chief intermediary for Comte's influence. Spencer does resemble Comte in many fundamental respects. Both men were positivists in their enthusiasm for the constant expansion of science into all phases of life. Both men devised similar hierarchies of the sciences and regarded sociology as particularly dependent on biology. Their similarities illustrate one of those frequent instances in the history of science in which men's own ideas are part of a complex of views gaining increasing currency in a period.

Early American sociologists were especially indebted to Comte and Spencer. They generally shared their positivistic fervor in endeavoring to extend science to the social sphere of life. Comte and Spencer also furnished the outlines of a conception of sociology as an evolutionary science which is a part, if not the apex of, an evolutionary hierarchy of sciences. American sociologists accepted Spencer's individualism but—aside from a few exceptions, notably Sumner—rejected his antivolitional biological determinism and laissez-faire doctrine. Sociology in the United States generally followed Comte's view of progress as susceptible of acceleration by purposive, rational intervention in society, though it denied his anti-individualistic organic notion of society. And early American sociologists were not hesitant to recognize their indebtedness to these and other British and Continental predecessors and contemporaries, with whom they often came in contact through travel or graduate work abroad.[4]

Basic Intellectual Characteristics

Nevertheless, the intellectual characteristics of American sociology are still manifestly American. Its problems, methods, assumptions, and preoccupations do reveal the distinctive impact of American society from the first books in the field after the Civil War, through the early sociology courses in the colleges and universities of the 188os and 189os, the volumes of the *American Journal of Sociology* beginning in 1896, and the official *Publications of the American Sociological Society* first issued in 1907.[5] The writings of the charter members of the American Sociological Society, which was organized in December, 1905 by a group of dissidents from the American Economic Association, reflect the American tenor of the discipline.

Throughout the years of the formative era four major characteristics of the sociological point of view prevailed. At the first official meeting of the American Sociological Society, held in Providence, Rhode Island in December, 1906, Albion W. Small presented a paper setting forth the points of agreement among sociologists.[6] His exposition as well as the comments by several discussants indicate that four assumptions were generally accepted at the beginning of the first period of American sociology.

Small pointed out that sociology, in its broadest sense, is an "inclusive and coordinated system of knowledge" about human relations. Even though this integrated system has not yet been achieved, sociologists must recognize the implicit "oneness of social knowledge" as a necessary assumption to guide their particular researches. This unity of knowledge is a corollary of the theory of evolution. Since all realms of nature which are studied by the presociological sciences of chemistry, physics, biology, and psychology contribute to the possibility of social relations, they are ultimately interrelated into the "oneness of social knowledge." Sociology's special task is the study of social relations (the associations of two or more individuals) which represent the highest level of evolution.

Investigation of social behavior, however, is not an end in itself. All knowledge should contribute to improving the lot of man, or as Small phrased it, must aid in the ultimate realization of the highest "spiritual possibilities of human beings" and the development of "higher types of human association." This moral and social progress is possible once man learns to control the resources and forces of the physical world and to use such knowledge to better mankind's material existence. Material progress, which should be equitably distributed among all men, is thus a precondition of moral progress. Nevertheless, both are assumed possible through human intervention based on scientific knowledge.

The laws of human association, which sociological investigations are to discover and formulate in order to promote social progress, explain both static social structures and dynamic social change *individualistically*. Thus sociological laws must conceive social phenomena as resulting from the dynamic nature of individual persons. "The structural or static phase of social occurrences is a sort of mirage," reasoned Small, because it is only a provisional representation of a tension of forces constantly rearranging itself and, consequently, never really static. In social change the same forces are operative. Although a small minority of sociologists still viewed these forces as biological in nature, the majority considered them to be essentially psychological. Apart from William G. Sumner, American sociologists generally rejected Comte's and Spencer's emphasis on the role of biology in social evolution.

Small specifically proposed that all social phenomena are fundamentally sentient acts of individuals. These acts, in turn, resolve themselves into the three elements of attention, valuation, and volition. Both social structure and change are to be explained by the aggregate similarities and dissimilarities of these psychic elements prevailing in the individual members of groups.

This conception of the ultimately psychic nature of the social realm led sociologists to agree that personality is their distinctive "center of attention" and "principle of synthesis." Consequently they studied the constitution of the personality and the process whereby it evolves in order to understand the past and future of human association.

In brief, Small confirmed the general acceptance of four major assumptions among American sociologists of 1906: (1) They accepted the task of searching for scientific laws of human behavior, which resemble invariant *natural laws* governing physical and organic phenomena. (2) They identified social change as social evolution and interpreted it as *progress* toward a better society. (3) They regarded such upward human development as subject to acceleration by direct human *melioristic intervention,* using knowledge of sociological laws. (4) Finally, they conceived of social behavior and society as constituted of *individual behavior* and particularly emphasized the motivations of individuals in association. Corroboration of the widespread acceptance of these major ideas by other sociologists during the remaining years of the formative period exists abundantly.

Belief in Natural Laws

Indeed at no time during the development of sociology has the existence of a system of fundamental, natural laws which govern the behavior of men been seriously questioned. During the early period this belief was encouraged by the Darwinian conception that men and animals evolved as part of the same developmental totality. As it was transplanted to the social realm by Herbert Spencer and William G. Sumner, the implicity deterministic nature of this position was not willingly accepted by American social thinkers committed to the tenet of individual volition so strongly stressed by Christianity. In order to avoid strict determinism, sociologists came in time to prefer and accept Lester F. Ward's viewpoint because it did not subordinate man completely to the invariant laws of nature. Ward agreed that man has evolved from the lower forms of life and is to that extent governed by natural laws, but he insisted that in the process of evolution man has acquired intellect and rationality with which he can attain a way of life above and apart from the natural world. In employing reason, man can acquire knowledge of the laws of human behavior; he can even learn to guide and direct the process of history and to create a better existence for himself.

While Sumner also believed in natural laws governing human behavior, he construed them so rigidly that little room was left for human intervention. Like the surrounding world of nature, man is part of an on-going system, culture. Into its stream he is born and subsequently he is molded by its folkways and mores which have been accumulated over centuries as the tested means of societal survival. Man, who is no different from other aspects of nature, is governed by the same invariant laws.

Franklin H. Giddings also interpreted social life as part of the larger realm of nature and as governed by natural laws which are to be ascertained. The most valid scientific conclusions about the nature and functioning of social life are to be obtained inductively, he argued, by quantitative procedures, especially statistics.

William I. Thomas and Florian Znaniecki set forth their belief in the existence of natural laws of human behavior in the Methodological Note of their classic work on *The Polish Peasant in Europe and America* (1918–1921). They noted that social change has proceded slowly in the earlier, simpler societies, but that with the conditions of life now undergoing rapid transition, man needs to learn to control and direct this change by discovering the laws of human behavior and applying them rationally for the improvement of the conditions of life. They therefore proposed an inductive, scientific approach for discovering these laws, and the case history as the most fruitful method in this undertaking.

During the period when American social thinkers were establishing an independent discipline of sociology they accepted the existence of universal laws of human behavior. Whether sociologists followed Sumner and Ward in deducing the lesser laws of social behavior from the broad, general laws of social process, or whether they preferred the more inductive methods of Giddings and Thomas, they agreed that the task of sociology is the scientific determination of the invariant, natural laws of human behavior.

Faith in Progressive Social Change

Operating teleologically, these laws were held to entail perpetual improvement of human welfare. Like the natural world, society began in simplicity—indeed, in moral poverty. As man evolved his social relations became more complex and man himself became increasingly rational. Eventually, the evolutionary process will lead man to higher levels of life at which human happiness and freedom will be ever greater.

This notion of social progress had its most immediate antecedents in the transformation of the conception of universal history at the close of the seventeenth century. In 1681 Bishop Bossuet wrote his *Discourse on Universal History* in which he reasserted St. Augustine's thesis that human events have moved through three epochs (the reign of nature, the reign of written law, and the reign of grace) in a divinely predestined course. Under the inspiration of Cartesian rationalism the Frenchman Turgot reformulated this account in more naturalistic terms. The epochs of events became the sequential stages of culture comprised of the conditions under which men live (the hunting, the pastoral, the agricultural, and the governmental stages). Providential design was replaced by a naturalistic cause-effect interpretation of accumulating knowledge. As knowledge accumulates through these several stages a desirable course of change termed *progress* is produced. Progressive change became a widely accepted article of faith among European intellectuals, and through Condorcet and Saint-Simon it was transmitted to Comte who incorporated it into sociology. The English exponents of this view, John Stuart Mill and Herbert Spencer, were particularly influential in spreading the doctrine of progress to the United States. In part because it was congenial with Christian notions of utopia and the millenial hope, was consistent with the Darwinian theory of natural evolution, and supplied an explanation of the social upheavals resulting from urbanization and industrialization, the doctrine of progress became part of American social thought. As in the case of the belief in the existence of invariant natural laws, no sociologist in the formative era disputed the belief in social progress. Ward even called himself an "apostle of human progress."

Ward's sociology was basically an optimistic, philosophical theory of social change. He posited three laws of social dynamics: (1) the potential of peoples and races to rise above their low state of culture; (2) innovation, the modifications stemming from mutation in biological reproduction; and (3) conation, the knowledge which leads to progress and happiness by means of informed public opinion and dynamic human action. Through the operation of these three laws, man's evolution from simpler forms of animal life has proceded by "sympodial development" and will progress until utopian existence is achieved.* If man's innate abilities are given adequate training, he can assist progress by utilizing the knowledge of the principles of social change in the planning of a better society and in the amelioration of current social evils and injustices. The importance which Ward attached to man's intervention in and acceleration of the social process is easily evident in his division of sociology into *pure,* or abstract, and *applied* sociology. The task of the former was said to be the determination and explication of the basic principles of social structure and social change, and that of the latter was "social telesis," or the conscious utilization of scientific principles in the attainment of a better society.

Edward C. Hayes, also an adherent of the idea of progress, believed that attainment of a better society is contingent upon the usage of scientific explanations of social causation. Sociology must provide such explanations, which should be undertaken on what Hayes called (following Comte) the *positivistic level* of knowledge. But sociologists, he held, were still operating on the metaphysical level in so far as their explanations—particularly those presented by Ward—were merely asserted relationships between social phenomena and social forces. Hayes believed that sociologists should determine the causal processes producing social phenomena because only then could they distinguish the social processes leading to the "good" from those leading to the "evil." By the exercise of power and control based on such knowledge, sociologists could then effectively aid the progress of civilization.

Perhaps the only prominent sociologist who did not subscribe without reservation to the belief in social progress was William G. Sumner. Most early sociologists combined the belief in progress with an acceptance of melioristic interventionism, using the former as a sanction for the latter. Sumner, however, argued vehemently against the humanitarianism and reformism of his colleagues and rejected the Spencerian identification of social evolution and social progress.

Based on the tenets of Malthus, Darwin, and Spencer, Sumner's theory of social evolution held that social development is a product of the natural laws of selection, adaptation, and transmission. Selection accounts for the physical survival of those people and races whose bodily strength permits them to struggle successfully with the forces of nature and with other societies; consequently, wars between *in-groups* and *out-groups* are creative forces in social change. Selection is also social, manifesting itself in economic success because the accumulation of wealth is possible only if men possess the economic virtues of industriousness, prudence, sobriety, and wisdom. If man would refrain from intervening in the natural process of selection, the weak members of society would die off and the human race would be constituted of the best and most virtuous. Human progress is thus basically moral progress, entailing the accumulation and transmission of acquired economic virtues. Since both crescive and enacted social institutions also operate according to the selective process. their functioning should not be subject to governmental interference.

---

* Ward borrowed the term *sympodial* from botany and used it to describe the continuous process of social development. When a major social form has grown and produced a secondary form, it discontinues its development. The secondary form then becomes the major one and in turn ceases to develop when it has produced a secondary development. This process continues until a *sociocracy* is achieved.

Adaptation, as a second necessary law of change, results from the pressure of economic forces and the tendency of man to seek maximization of pleasure. The term *folkways* refers in general to group behavior patterns which contribute to adaptation, but *mores* are conventionalized ways whereby the members of society have successfully adapted themselves, rationally and irrationally, to their various environments. Moreover, all three types—mores of maintenance, perpetuation, and gratification—are patterns of behavior viewed by members of the in-group as essential to group welfare.

The last law of social change is transmission from one generation to the next, both biologically, by means of man's instinctual equipment, and culturally, by means of mythology. If a laissez-faire policy is followed, these laws of social development operate naturally and the quality of human existence improves. But Sumner was pessimistic about the inevitability of human progress because reform activities interfered with the functioning of the natural process in the name of humanitarianism. Thus he accepted and explained the laws of social evolution, although he was too realistic about human intervention to suppose that these laws would be permitted to achieve a happier, freer, and better society.

Social Reformism

The third basic assumption of early American sociology was the acceptance of melioristic intervention. Clear illustration of this early reformism is found in the books and articles dealing with one selected social problem or social problems in general. Including many men recruited by sociology from a variety of fields and with diverse and special interests, the list of sociologists committed to meliorism is extensive.[7]

For example, Charles E. Ellwood's once popular text, *Sociology and Modern Social Problems*, interrelates the acceptance of melioristic interests with the other presuppositions of natural law, progress, and individualism. Ellwood assumed both the inevitability of the process of social evolution and the ultimate attainment through social progress of a society characterized by harmonious adjustments among individuals, by efficiency of members in performing their social roles, and by social survival. Sociology was to assist in the achievement of these ideal social conditions by developing and applying scientific knowledge about social organization and social evolution. For the problems of industrialization and urbanization, sociology itself was to be a kind of general social reform. Because urbanization is a necessary and irreversible part of evolution, realistic amelioration of its undesirable conditions requires modifications progressing in the same direction as the main process of change. Such reform would be fundamentally sound only if it attacks the basic difficulty which rests not in biological factors nor in governmental procedures, but in the patterned behavior and moral character of individuals. The best remedy for the evils of city life—divorce, crime, insanity, suicide, poverty, illegitimacy, and racial and minority problems—is the education of the young. This training is to be based on the norms and behavior which sociology would discover as most adequate to the new urban way of life. Meliorism is thus to proceed according to sociological principles and to educate the young to a higher level of intelligence and morality.

Sociologists differed about the appropriate role of the state in melioristic intervention. Opposing viewpoints are particularly apparent in the works of Sumner and Ward. According to Sumner, any extension of the responsibilities of government threatens the efficient fulfilment of its primary function of providing citizens with peace, order, and security. Furthermore, the state is essentially a political power and often the instrument which social classes employ to advance their own special interests. The benefits accruing from governmental intervention are accordingly distributed predominantly to members of the social class in control of the state, while the burdens rest disproportionately with members of other classes. Finally, the natural process of evolution operates best without individual or governmental interference. Consequently, the only legislative reform to which Sumner ever gave his outright approval was free trade, which proposes to permit economic intercourse among nations to proceed according to the so-called natural law of competition. In almost all other legislative programs, Sumner saw misplaced, superficial efforts to accelerate the social process. True progress could and would occur only gradually in accordance with the free operation of its own natural laws.

Ward never shared Sumner's distrust of the state. A paleobotanist in the United States Civil Service for many years, he believed that a truly representative form of government existed in the United States. He rejected the notion that the state is a tool of any one social class. In contrast, he considered the state as the necessary medium for the expression of the popular will; he applauded the increase in regulatory legislation, seeking only to make such laws more scientific and rational. Therefore he approved the government's collection of statistics. Furthermore, it seemed contradictory to Ward that there should be such widespread commendation of the desirability of the scientific control of natural phenomena while a laissez-faire policy was upheld in the social realm. Nature is wasteful in both the biological and social spheres. Just as man has already benefited from the control of physical and biological phenomena, he can now hope for similar and even greater advantages from the scientific control and purposive guidance of his social relations. Since the state operates in the interest of the general welfare, it must become an increasingly more important controlling agency in society in order to fulfil the needs and purposes of the majority. The hope of civilization, therefore, rests in the allocation of ever more activities to the state and in the creation of a *sociocracy*—a democratic society governed rationally by all its citizens.

Edward A. Ross, like his contemporaries, was greatly interested in the continuity of the social process and in social reform. He championed a large variety of reform proposals, particularly programs to promote the well-being of labor and the freedom of thought and speech. Sociologists, he held, should study the three phases of the social process: the preliminary process, which is not in fact social, the social, and the reconstructive process. The last is crucial since it prevents the products of the social process—institutions, uniformities, imperatives, groups, and social relations —from becoming static. The basic or "over-mastering purpose" of sociology, however, is the improvement of human relations.[8] As a result of his own world-wide travels, Ross's melioristic inclinations were characterized by an unusually broad and international scope. Throughout his investigations he stressed the interrelatedness of the economic forces and social justice (or injustice) and their joint effect on social movements. After he had personally investigated revolts and revolutions in many parts of the world, particularly China, Mexico, and Russia, he concluded that class exploitation must be eliminated if real social progress is to persist.

Moreover, Ross insisted that the process of social change from community to society requires greater knowledge and awareness of the means of social control in the modern world. Discovering the principles of social control is a major problem for sociology, and Ross himself was the first American sociologist to publish a book on this topic.[9] Once they have been formulated, however, the principles of social control should not be accessible to all members of the society equally and without qualification, according to Ross. Rather the "wise sociologist" should make such knowledge available only to the guardians of morality—the teachers, clergymen, editors, lawmakers, and judges—in order that exploitation and misuse for private power and gain will not result. Yet Ross considered an intelligent, dynamic public opinion based on scientific knowledge of social organization one of the greatest aids to social progress and he therefore wrote many books, often in a lively, muckraking style, to popularize sociological knowledge.

He believed—as did Ward, uncle of his first wife—that the state is a potentially useful agency in human society. Particularly in a democracy in which no one social class exercises exclusive control, the state is the most appropriate medium for expressing community interests and improving human welfare. Thus, he concluded that most social reform should eventually proceed through the state, a notion fundamentally similar to Ward's hope for a sociocracy in which well-educated citizens run their affairs happily and intelligently. Ross made some changes in his thinking as sociology developed during the first half of the twentieth century, but he never relinquished this belief that the basic purpose of sociology is the offering of guidance and assistance in the reform of human relationships.

Individualistic Conception of Society

Throughout the last half-century American sociologists have adhered to an individualistic conception of social life. They have generally viewed all social groups as pluralities of associating and interacting individuals whose psychic nature is the ultimate source of social change. Sociologists of the formative era already accepted this viewpoint, as the earlier reference to Small's article indicates. Accordingly, many early American sociologists rejected Comte's conception that the historical process had made society something more than the mere sum of its individual members.

Since early sociologists were so deeply preoccupied with social change, their individualistic presuppositions are most clearly evident in their search for the dynamic sources of social evolution. Joined by social philosophers and psychologists, they traced social experience to elementary human motives, referring to them variously as social forces, interests, and instincts. After a detailed study of the social forces concept, one authority concludes that the formative era of American sociology is best described as the period "when the social forces and instinct concepts were dominant."[10]

Ward was the first sociologist to set forth an orderly classification of these universal tendencies of human nature. In *Dynamic Sociology* (1883) and in *Pure Sociology* (1903) he proposed that feeling is the dynamic force in the sympodial development of social evolution. The psychic force of feeling manifests itself in desires, the strongest of which are hunger and love. Ward classified these desires under two major headings: physical forces which concern bodily functions, and spiritual forces which pertain to psychic functions. Physical forces are in turn divided into the onto-genetic, or those seeking pleasure and avoiding pain, and the phylogenetic, or those pertaining to direct or sexual desires and to indirect or consan-guineal ones. Spiritual forces are all sociogenetic and include moral, es-thetic, and intellectual motives. These forces, which embody the dynamic impulses of all human achievement, assume their peculiarly social nature in the process of human interaction and association. It is significant that Ward's concept of social forces incorporates a kind of conative or voli-tional tendency which insures the human spirit against complete absorp-tion into the system of universal natural laws.

Even Sumner, who held to his notion of cultural determinism almost dogmatically, and who disagreed—often bitterly—with Ward, was essen-tially individualistic in his sociology. He viewed the current conditions of society, particularly the relative positions of economic classes, as the result of successful and unsuccessful competition of individuals in the struggle for survival. The poor are at the bottom of the social ladder because as in-dividuals they lack those personal virtues which make for economic suc-cess. The social process and human evolution are also ultimately the out-come of the activities of individuals, specifically as they are motivated by the instincts of hunger, sex love, vanity, and ghost fear. These fundamental drives are responsible for human survival and the creation of civilization because they encourage men to develop, by trial and error, group habits or folkways which are best suited to satisfy these needs. Moreover, the process of satisfying these irrational human tendencies effects the development of certain human interests. For example, hunger led to interest in the develop-ment of tools and weapons and the acquisition of wealth; sex love encour-aged the development of sex mores and the institution of the family; vanity was the moving force behind the preoccupation with beauty; and fear led to the concern with supernatural powers, ghosts, and spirits. In short, society is organized in its present form as the consequence of the personal characteristics of its individual members. The social process is the outcome of the operation of basic motives of human nature which lead to the creation of folkways and thereby facilitate man's successful participa-tion in the struggle for survival.

The individualistic assumptions of early sociology similarly inhere in Small's classification of *interests*. Small used as his point of departure the theory of the Austrian sociologist Gustav Ratzenhofer who held that the elements of the human associational process and the bases for the estab-lishment of human institutions are interests within individuals. According to Small, these interests, which prompt man to action, are of six types: health, wealth, sociability, knowledge, beauty, and rightness. There is little difference between Small's notion of interests and Ward's theory of social forces, for both function as elemental motives producing social change and human association. Small considered the social process, or what Ward called *social evolution*, as the product of the two subprocesses of social conflict and cooperation which are prompted by conflicting or corresponding interests respectively. Since sociology is obligated to study social evolution in order to promote a more adequate social order, it must investigate human associations in terms of these elementary interests. Perhaps because of its greater simplicity and possibly because of Small's many years of extensive contact with students at the University of Chicago, his formulation of interests found more widespread acceptance in sociological circles than Ward's theory of social forces.

In the writings of Giddings there is a somewhat different expression of individualism. Urging the use of the inductive method of statistics in the search for the laws of social evolution, Giddings assumed that society is a kind of mathematical sum of its separate units. The units are individuals in interaction. Interaction is essentially the outcome of that state of consciousness which leads both high and low forms of life to recognize a species like itself—a fundamental and primitive awareness or *consciousness of kind*. As mankind evolved and social life became more complex, man experienced greater difficulty in recognizing others like himself. But consciousness of kind is an essential element in the attainment of true progress, and should therefore be developed, controlled, and guided so that like-minded men will associate freely and voluntarily for their own welfare. By promoting consciousness of kind, sociology can facilitate the establishment of a more ideal society. Thus society is not only viewed as an association of individuals, but the ideal society is one in which like-mindedness of men encourages association within the larger group and various subgroups.

This individualistic and psychological orientation to the study of society can be amply documented from the works of other major and minor figures in sociology. For instance, Ross's textbook in social psychology embodied both Ward's notion of social forces and Small's classification of interests. In volumes by Ellwood, Blackmar, Gillin, Bushee, and others the notion of social forces reappeared. This individualism, as we have called it, of American sociology has given the field a kind of unity which has persisted and has integrated the field in spite of its many controversies about methods and purposes. American sociology has traditionally viewed society as the sum of individuals who are, in turn, the source of all that is produced in and characteristic of the society.

Arising at a time of industrialization, early sociology concerned itself primarily with the scientific study and amelioration of social problems in urban areas. The founders of sociology, with their generally nonurban and nonsecular experiences, were particularly sensitive to these problems which they interpreted as accompaniments of social progress. The theories of Comte and Spencer, and the singular absence of major national crises after the Civil War were conducive to the interpretation of social change as progress. The upheaval of World War I, as the next chapter will show, affected the second period more than the first: it altered the belief in progress, the direct interest in meliorism, the study of human nature, and the conception of scientific sociology.

Just as certain intellectual and social antecedents were significant for early sociology, so the character of sociology in its formative period is crucial for the state of the discipline today (1954). Developments since the first era have usually been modifications and refinements of earlier problems, methods, scope, and assumptions. Thus, the explicit endorsement of meliorism has been replaced by a more subtle instrumentalism; scientific procedures and techniques have been specialized, differentiated, and elaborated; and knowledge of the development and operation of human motivation, which is still held to determine social behavior, social structure, and social change, has become more detailed.

Footnotes to Chapter One

1. This statement is exemplified by the careers of Lester F. Ward, William G. Sumner, Franklin H. Giddings, Albion W. Small, Edward A. Ross, George E. Vincent, George E. Howard, Charles H. Cooley, Frank W. Blackmar, James Q. Dealey, Edward C. Hayes, James P. Lichtenberger, Ulysses G. Weatherly, Charles A. Ellwood, Robert E. Park, John L. Gillin, William I. Thomas, John M. Gillette, and Frank H. Hankins. For further readings on the lives and contributions of these sociologists see especially Odum, Howard W.: *American Sociology*, New York, Longmans, Green and Co., Inc., 1951.

2. Bernard, L. L., and Jessie Bernard: *Origins of American Sociology*, New York, Thomas Y. Crowell Co., 1943.

3. *Ibid.*, pp. 637–638, 657–667.

4. Among other influential Europeans were John Stuart Mill, Alfred R. Wallace, Charles Darwin, Walter Bagehot, Gabriel Tarde, Gustav Ratzenhofer, Ludwig Gumplowicz, Wilhelm Wundt, Ferdinand Toennies, Georg Simmel, Gustav Schmoller, Albert Schaeffle, and Wilhelm Windelband.

5. The first volume of these reports of the American Sociological Society was printed in 1907 and included the papers and discussions of the first meeting held in December, 1906. Officially, Volumes I through IX are entitled *Papers and Proceedings of the American Sociological Society*. In 1916, beginning with Volume X, the title was changed to *Publications of the American Sociological Society*, although the former title remained as a subtitle. For the sake of consistency the title *Publications of the American Sociological Society* will be used throughout the present study.

6. Small, Albion W.: "Points of Agreement among Sociologists," *Publications of the American Sociological Society* I:55–71 (1907).

7. Both major and minor figures, many of whom had strong religious inclinations, were involved, for instance: Luther L. Bernard, Frank W. Blackmar, Frederick A. Bushee, James Q. Dealey, Edward T. Devine, Edwin L. Earp, Charles A. Ellwood, John M. Gillette, John L. Gillin, Ernest R. Groves, James E. Hagerty, Charles R. Henderson, Maurice Parmelee, and Marion Talbot.

8. Page, Charles Hunt: *Class and American Sociology: From Ward to Ross*, New York, Dial Press, 1940, p. 241.

9. Ross, Edward Alsworth: *Social Control*, New York, The Macmillan Co., 1926, especially pp. 395–442.

10. House, Floyd Nelson: *The Development of Sociology*, New York, McGraw-Hill Book Co., Inc., 1936, p. 243.

chapter two

The Quest to Make Sociology Scientific (1918–1935)

|||||||||||||||||||||||||||||||||||||||||||||||||||||||||||||||||||||||||||||||||||||||||||||||||||||||||||||||||||||||||||||||||||||||||||||||||||||||||||||||||||||||||||

Both as an academic profession and a scientific discipline, sociology probably changed more rapidly and more extensively during the period between the end of World War I and the Depression than at any other time. The expansion of the college and university student population largely made possible the upsurge in the recruitment of sociologists. Consequently, the number of newer members in the American Sociological Society quickly exceeded the older generation. In teaching and research a professional division of labor was established as sociologists confined themselves to the more or less permanent specialized fields then developing. The growing stature of sociology as a science was indicated by frequent participation of sociologists in interdisciplinary ventures. Within sociology, efforts to make the scientific foundation more secure led to a preoccupation with a series of methodological problems.

During these years the research, theorization, and graduate instruction at the University of Chicago gave its Department of Sociology an unprecedented preeminence in sociology. Any understanding of the major trends during this second period of sociology's development is impossible without consideration of the Chicago contribution in the fields of social psychology, urban sociology, ethnic and race relations, social change, and statistics. But the quest to make sociology scientific was, indeed, the pervasive endeavor, as a more extended examination of the features of this period discloses.

Professional Expansion

Since sociology's existence, then as now, depends almost wholly upon its fortune as a subject to be taught to college students, the increase in the college enrollments during the 1920s was a fact of great importance for sociology. By 1930 the general college-student population was twice the 1920 figure of 462,445. Moreover, the increase in the number of basic sociology textbooks intended for undergraduates, from 10 in the decade 1910–1919 to 26 in the decade 1920–1929, suggests that sociology maintained its popularity among college students.

At the same time more students enrolled for graduate training. The number of graduate students trebled from 1920 to 1930; the number of graduate degrees increased threefold from 1918 to 1924; and the number of Ph.D. degrees awarded in 1930 was four times the 1920 figure. The *American Journal of Sociology*'s annual listings of sociology Ph.D. dissertations in progress indicated that sociology shared in the increasing numbers of graduate students.

These expanded undergraduate and graduate enrollments coincided with some of the principal changes in the American Sociological Society. First, the membership of the Society expanded rapidly during the 1920s. Beginning with 115 members in 1906, it gradually attained a membership plateau of some 700 persons throughout the war years, 1915–1919. During the next decade, 1919–1929, the increase from 852 to 1812 amounted to 113 per cent. Second, a younger generation of sociologists already outnumbered the founding generation of the Society. Although 70 per cent of the older generation who had been members in 1910 were still associated with the Society in 1917, they then comprised only 12 per cent of the total membership. Third, sectional dominance of the Society passed to the academic institutions of the Middle West in this same period. Based on the proportion of the total membership of the Society, the Middle West wrested from the East in 1919 a leadership retained throughout the 1920s.*

The Middle West also acquired dominance in terms of the percentage of papers contributed at annual meetings. From 1918 to 1929 it had about 51 per cent of the papers as opposed to the East's 37 per cent, whereas in the earlier years, 1906–1918, the East and the Middle West had each presented about 48 per cent of the papers. Of the Middle Western contributions made during the 1920s, moreover, about 70 per cent came from representatives of a limited number of academic institutions: University of Chicago and the state universities in Wisconsin, Minnesota, North Dakota, Ohio, Kansas, Michigan, and Missouri. In contrast, fewer Eastern papers, only about 60 per cent, came from a greater number of educational institutions. Columbia, Cornell, Yale, Pennsylvania, Brown, and Smith College were the most frequently involved. About 40 per cent of the Eastern papers were delivered by persons from governmental agencies, foundations, and miscellaneous organizations and professional schools.[1]

Sociology, then, expanded rapidly after World War I. A younger generation of Middle Western and academically affiliated sociologists assumed a dominant position in sociology.

Emergence of Special Fields

Concurrently, sociologists began to specialize their interests and, accordingly, delimited fields of endeavor appeared. The first official recognition of emergent subject differentiation in sociology occurred in 1921. E. C. Hayes, who was president of the Society that year, inaugurated a change in policy in the organization of the annual program. No longer were all of the papers necessarily solicited only as they could be focused around one

---

* The previous observation (see Chapter One) that 15 of the 19 presidents of the American Sociological Society, born prior to 1880, graduated by 1910, and prominent before 1920 had in some way been associated with the Middle West, does not refute this fact. The leadership of the Middle West during the second period of American sociology involved not only the highest ranking professional men but the rank and file of sociologists doing research and teaching in Midwestern institutions.

central problem or topic. Under the new policy the program was prepared by committees, each of which had charge of a special subdivision such as social evolution, biological factors in social causation, or psychic factors in social causation, and round-table discussions were introduced which dealt with such varied topics as delinquency, education and research, community problems, rural neighborhood units, and social work. As the decade advanced, titles of the subject divisions and the topics selected for round-table discussions were changed.

Closer inspection of these subject fields suggests that they crystallized around the social problems toward which melioristic interest had been directed during the formative period. Though the traditions of progress and meliorism were formally rejected as accepted intellectual justifications for sociological activity during these years, they did bequeath to sociology a utilitarian emphasis which continued to encourage the accumulation of knowledge applicable to concrete problems of the social order. The trend to make sociology more scientific similarly stimulated field differentiation and specialization, for being scientific was generally construed to mean engaging in concrete research. Effective prosecution of research meant, in turn, the delimitation of problems and their specific incorporation within a major specialty of the larger sociological discipline. The list of principal fields within sociology thus reveals concern either with problems of race and population, community, rural and urban conditions, social psychology, family, social work, social change, criminology, educational sociology, folk sociology and religion, or with questions pertaining to social research methods, statistics, general theory, and history of social thought.

Interdisciplinary Cooperation

However differentiated their fields of inquiry and however specialized their interests might have become, sociologists did not withdraw generally from the broader social science domain. Their participation in a variety of interdisciplinary ventures suggests that their colleagues in other fields respected and recognized them as members of a distinct, social-scientific discipline. Indeed, participation of sociologists actually functioned to heighten the independence of sociology as a separate social science, with its own viewpoint and its own body of knowledge.

Formed in 1923 by representatives from economics, political science, sociology, and statistics as a means of furthering joint research by members of the various social sciences and of establishing an adequate scientific methodology, the Social Science Research Council was one of the first of such interdisciplinary projects. Of the two purposes mentioned, the development of a scientific methodology was especially important because it encouraged utilization of several scientific methods in the exploration of specific problems. Two of the original three representatives from the American Sociological Society—Stuart Chapin, William Ogburn, and Shelby Harrison—were statistically oriented, a viewpoint in keeping with the stress on scientific achievement through quantification in sociology. The *Encyclopedia of the Social Sciences*, which was published in 1934, was another venture requiring cooperation from all of the social sciences. At various times in its preparation, Alexander Goldenweiser, William Ogburn, and

W. I. Thomas represented sociology. Other interdisciplinary ventures included the round-table discussions at the annual meetings which involved particularly the collaboration of sociologists, social workers, economists, and psychiatrists. There were also symposia on the state of the social sciences, their activities, and methods, to which sociologists as well as other social scientists contributed. One of the best known of these was *Recent Developments in the Social Sciences*, edited by E. C. Hayes and published in 1927.[2]

Shifts in Rationale

Some of this recognition which was accorded sociology with the participation of its representatives in interdisciplinary ventures was certainly the result of sociologists' rigorous efforts to apply the scientific method to their discipline. Yet the concern with scientific method, so characteristic of this era of sociology, seems to have been occasioned, in part, by the impact of World War I on the rationale for carrying on sociological inquiry.

World War I was accompanied by a pervasive revision of the intellectual justification for science. Previously, sociologists had shared in the prevailing American belief that man is essentially rational, by virtue of which a faith in science and progress is encouraged, if not guaranteed. As man's intellect makes possible technical and material progress, so social-scientific knowledge, it was held, advances society in harmony with humanitarian ideals and thereby assures moral progress.

But the implications of the war severely shook the intellectuals' faith in progress. To a people whose belief "in progress had fathered the conviction that war among civilized powers was an anachronism," World War I was a shocking disappointment. Such violence symbolized a primitive stage of social evolution which modern man was believed to have passed long ago. Many sociologists concurred with other intellectuals in concluding that man is not essentially rational. Human nature is irrational, dominated by emotional predispositions! "Human nature, the war has taught us," lamented Ernest H. Groves in 1920, "has changed little since the time of primitive man . . ."[3] In 1924 U. G. Weatherly decried Ward's glorification of rationalism as false, since the war had revealed human nature to be as irrational today as it had been in prehistoric times.[4]

Sociologists thus became pessimistic about progressive improvements which had heretofore been regarded as the inevitable products of man's rationality. The predominance of irrationality in human nature made progress improbable if not altogether illusory. On occasion this pessimism was formulated in terms of the differential rate of change between material culture and morality; science and technology were viewed as developing too rapidly for man's nature which had remained primarily primitively emotional. Groves interpreted the social discontent of the early 1920s as the consequence of the disparity between the rate of change in science and an essentially primitive, nonrational human nature—a condition symptomatic of the cessation of progress. Weatherly regarded the lag between the primitiveness of human dispositions and the complexity and specialization of the techniques for satisfying wants as likely to destroy progress. Ellwood believed progress is difficult or perhaps impossible in an intolerant society,

for intolerance, a manifestation of irrationality, discourages adaptive innovation and prohibits intercommunication and public discussion of new
ideas and policies.

Concern with Scientific Method

Many younger sociologists were inclined to conclude that if human behavior is primarily a result of the operation of nonrational forces, sociology
should seek to determine the laws whereby these forces operate. Both the
scarcity of knowledge about such laws and the prevailing quest to make
sociology as scientific as other, more mature social science disciplines encouraged the increase of scientific research about these forces of human
nature. As research was undertaken sociologists became much more aware
of the methodological prerequisites of scientific method and the need to
reassess their own principles of inquiry. In particular, they became conscious of (1) the need for sociology to deal inductively with empirical,
concrete phenomena, (2) the importance of multicausational, rather than
particularistic, explanations, (3) the relative merits of the statistical and
life-history methods, and (4) the subjective-objective distinction with respect to scientific viewpoints and scientific data.

Preference for Concrete, Empirical Research

After World War I sociologists generally came to appreciate inductive
scientific procedures. In the formative period the prevalence of broad
philosophies of history had encouraged an unrecognized deductivism: more
delimited and specific principles of social life were derived from comprehensive, a priori laws of history. However, the war provoked widespread
skepticism of the most commonly employed, general, deductive progressive
law—social evolution. The rejection of this "speculative theory" and the
acceptance of the more advanced and concretely-oriented social and natural
sciences as models for sociology contributed to the disrepute of deductivism
and the ascendance of careful description and comparative analysis of
actual behavior—the basic requirements of induction. Consistent with this
newer inductive emphasis, Small suggested in 1921 that the analysis of
groups should begin with their "immediately presented factual phases."[5]
The following year Ogburn stressed the usefulness of the historical method
in securing "cultural facts" by which the reliability of social and social
psychological phenomena could be established.[6] A few years later Luther
L. Bernard similarly affirmed the necessity for investigating and understanding limited social events and behavior before the laws of larger processes
could be formulated and known.[7]

The preference for induction and concrete empirical data can be illustrated by the debacle of the doctrine of instincts. Although this significant
development in the realm of social psychology did not culminate until
1924 with the publication of Bernard's critical study of instincts, it was
greatly advanced by Ellsworth Faris in 1921 and 1922.[8] In an article in
which he contraposed "data" and "hypotheses" Faris noted that "the mis-
take of thinking that hypotheses are data" had led most psychologists and
sociologists to a misuse of the instinct concept. It was his contention that

instincts are not data: "human instincts are explanatory assumptions and not observable phenomena." Moreover, both the existing classifications of instincts are in a state of confusion and the elaborate accounts of social origins are frequently pure speculation because they assume universal, innate instincts which cannot be observed and verified.

In support of this viewpoint about the hypothetical nature of instincts, Faris cited ethnological evidence which he had either collected himself during his years in Africa or obtained from published anthropological sources. He indicated that the explanation for the great diversity of customs among contemporary noncivilized and civilized peoples cannot be derived from a limited number of universal psychic elements such as instincts. Rather, the peculiar local social circumstances are significant; they likewise condition personality development and variation in different societies. Consequently, since scientific knowledge about both cultural diversity and personality formation cannot be based on hypothetical instincts, concrete empirical research into specific social conditions is required.

In this connection Faris also rejected generalizations based on a kind of analogical reasoning. Many social psychologists interpreted the behavior of prehistoric man to be simple and therefore a relatively unmodified expression of the instincts. Since children's, neurotics', and contemporary non-civilized peoples' actions also seemed to be direct expressions of instincts, their behavior was often explained by employing the speculations about prehistoric man. But Faris insisted that "primitive man who is really primitive is gone and gone forever." Since "none of us ever saw him alive," his behavior will always remain unknown. If scientific knowledge about the actions of children, neurotics, or contemporary primitives is desired, it must be obtained through observation and investigation, rather than by analogizing and speculating about primitive ancestors.

Invoking ethnological data and the need for empirical study, Faris thus reappraised and rejected the classifications of instincts, theories of social origins which assume instincts, and analogical reasoning about behavior. Students of social psychology, he concluded, should turn away from the error of regarding instincts as observable and classifiable data and "should build on a foundation of facts."

Preference for Multicausational Explanations

Another post World War I trend in sociology was the increasing tendency to accept multicausational (pluralistic or multiple-factor) explanations and to reject monocausational (single-factor, monistic, or particularistic) interpretations. Though particularistic explanations seem to have received censure even during the years before World War I, certain conditions which favored single-factor interpretations existed. Certain early sociologists were inclined to attribute exclusive importance to the factors associated with their previous academic background and specialty, such as economics, biology, geography. Their adherence to evolutionary theory, with the possibility of undue emphasis on any of its different levels—from the physical, chemical, biological, psychic, to the social itself—was also conducive to particularism.

Although sociologists during the decade of the 1920s continued to locate the ultimate source of human behavior in the psychic nature of man, they came to accept the necessary presence and interplay of other factors. Accordingly, their generalizations and explanations were multicausational or pluralistic, encompassing relevant factors from all levels of existence. William I. Thomas and Cecil North are exemplary of this multiple-factor orientation. Thomas' situational approach views the behavior of individuals as the interactive product of wishes, attitudes, and values within a given set of environmental conditions. North employed both biological factors, such as age, sex, race, and individual differences, and social factors, such as privilege, accommodation, and status, to explain social differentiation.[9]

Preference for a multiple-factor approach was revealed in both general methodological articles and in standards of criticism employed in evaluating research. Thus, for example, Hayes forewarned in 1922 that "the vice of particularism which besets all social sciences" must be avoided if sociology is to become entirely scientific.[10]

The Case Study—Statistics Controversy

Polemics over the merits of case-study and statistical techniques is probably the best-known expression of the concerns with scientific method in this period. The proponents of the respective techniques held fundamentally different conceptions of the crux of scientific procedure. While protagonists of statistics accepted quantification and correlation, their case-study antagonists insisted rather that an understanding of the *total* individual, group, institution, or community, and a determination of causal processes were required.

Though it was first accepted slowly, the life-history technique, which became the best-known form of the case-study method, was extensively used by 1930. Employing personal documents, such as letters, autobiographies, and case records in their investigation of the social and personal organization and disorganization, William I. Thomas and Florian Znaniecki, in *The Polish Peasant in Europe and America*, successfully introduced the technique to sociologists. William Healy had been one of the first to point out the advantages of the life-history method to sociologists; by its use, he proposed, scientific sociology can rectify its lack of factual knowledge about man's inner, mental life. By 1929 a total of 75 articles and books in sociology dealing with life histories had been published. They disclosed a general agreement that the life history is "an account of the life of a person presented in such a manner that the development of habits and attitudes may be traced. The term implies a complete account of all phases of life."

Although the case-study method was used more frequently in the study of individuals, it is also applicable to the investigation of groups, institutions, and communities. Its application to communities resulted, in part, from the extension of an earlier interest in social surveys, such as Charles Booth's *Life and Labor of the People of London* (1892–1897), Paul U. Kellogg's *The Pittsburgh Survey* (1909–1914), and Shelby Harrison's *The Springfield Survey* (1918). Sociological study of communities was also encouraged by sociologists' contacts with anthropological accounts of "whole cultures" of nonliterate societies. One of the best-known case studies em-

ploying this holistic approach in the study of the culture and social structure of a community is Robert S. and Helen M. Lynd's two-volume *Middletown* (1929) and *Middletown in Transition* (1937). These studies have
stimulated much subsequent community research.

Sociologists attributed certain advantages and disadvantages to the case-
study method, especially the life history. Its proponents claimed that it is
an inductive method because it begins with the accumulation of concrete
data. Focusing on qualitative interrelations, it can discover causal sequences, processes of change in time, and complex mechanisms of interrelationships of social phenomena. By virtue of viewing social phenomena
as a whole, it reveals the dynamics of personality development.

The primary disadvantages of this method stem from its subjectivism.
On the one hand, the reliability of the memory or the accessibility of the
motivation of the person being studied is open to question. On the other,
the personal biases and preferences of the investigator can intrude into the
interpretation of data.

Statistical procedures were often advanced because they avoided such
subjectivism. Those who championed quantitative research procedures
sometimes associated scientific method exclusively with the precision and
reliability of their technique. Special discussions on statistical sociology at
the annual meetings and the personal efforts of such scholars as Franklin
H. Giddings, F. Stuart Chapin, William F. Ogburn, Stuart A. Rice, and
John Gillin familiarized sociologists with the desirability of the use of statistical techniques. By 1929 a group of sociologists, many of whom have
since become prominent, envisioned the future trends in American sociology as a constant expansion and strengthening of the quantitative orientation.[11]

The case for statistics was presented vigorously. Its proponents insisted
that sociology will command a status commensurate with that of other
sciences only by using the common credential of scientific respectability—
quantification. Statistical conclusions are precise, verifiable, valid, useful in
prediction, less elaborate, less costly than those arrived at by qualitative
methods, such as life histories, and finally, are objective in that they cannot be biased by prejudiced interpretations of the data.

Opponents reminded statisticians of the limitations of their research tool.
They contended statistics cannot express causal sequences or mechanisms
but only cross-sectional views; they cannot reveal dynamics of action but
only the presence or absence of selected factors; they cannot describe an
entity as a whole; and they can never reach the inner, subjective elements
in the mental life of man.

The occasional reappearance of the statistics-case study debate in current
sociological discussions is evidence that a complete solution was never
achieved. In the later 1920s and early 1930s certain sociologists, including
Read Bain and Kimball Young, suggested a resolution of the controversy
by recommending the use of both techniques in sociological analysis.[12]

The Subjectivism—Objectivism Controversy

The resolution of the statistics-case method controversy contained two
postulates which were themselves developed in the course of other preoccu-

pations concerning procedures of scientific inquiry. On the one hand, sociologists accepted the desirability of scientific objectivity and, on the other, they consented to the inclusion of certain subjective phenomena as data for sociological research. The separate disputes which gave rise to these two propositions unfortunately employed the identical terminology of subjectivism and objectivism in different contexts, creating widespread confusion in the meanings of these terms.

One subjectivism-objectivism distinction referred to the proper relationships of the researcher's own values to his problem and data of investigation. When a scientist pursued his problem without introducing his own biases, prejudices, or preferences, he was said to be proceeding "objectively"; contrariwise, when these personal values affected his work, he was said to be "subjective." Thus William Ogburn rejected both social theory and social philosophy as subjective because they are mere personal rationalizations or wishful thinking resulting from emotional biases and speculative hunches;[13] Stuart Rice insisted that sociology must be free from value judgments and deal with values only if they are data of analysis;[14] and similarly, Henry P. Fairchild indicated that sociologists as scientists must not inject their own values and goals, but must limit themselves to demonstrating how to attain the ends set by the society.[15] By the early 1930s sociologists generally agreed that research should be conducted objectively; researchers should proceed without value judgments or personal preferences concerning the utilization of knowledge.

Concurrently a second issue pertaining to a distinction between subjectivism and objectivism arose. At first this controversy was fairly distinct from the question of biased or value-laden perspectives on the part of the researcher. It pertained primarily to the kind of data which sociologists should investigate. Accordingly, in its early phases it was associated with the statistics-case method controversy and the evaluation of behaviorism.

Behaviorists and statisticians tended to agree that the data of science should be objective and include only observable, quantifiable, and verifiable material. Strict behaviorism excludes the concepts of consciousness, subconsciousness, will, feeling, wishes, mind, or self because they refer to phenomena which are subjective, internal, nonobservable, and therefore neither accessible nor verifiable scientifically.

Although many sociologists were favorably disposed toward behaviorism, and some were frequently identified with this approach, no major figure in the field accepted behaviorism completely. Directly or indirectly they always attributed the final force in society and culture to man's inner, nonphysical, and mental life.* In the sociological writings attacking behaviorism this implicit acceptance of the significance of subjective factors in social behavior is most articulate. Charles Ellwood, for example, declared that the crucial question of behaviorism is whether or not "subjective terms have a legitimate place in the social sciences. . . ." Because behaviorism excludes the possibility of the scientific study of attitudes, values, motives, and desires of individuals and groups, he concluded, it is methodologically in error and prevents a thorough understanding of human behavior.[16]

Like Ellwood, Robert MacIver stressed the legitimacy of subjective

---

* This qualification of behaviorism is consistent with the voluntaristic nominalism which has been a basic postulate of American sociology from the beginning.

phenomena in sociology and regarded an exclusive concern with objective, measurable data as "wholly mistaken."[17] MacIver, expanding the subjectivist position, distinguished between an "inner system of reality" and "outer system." Knowledge of the inner, which includes the subjective factors of social behavior, he maintained, is absolutely essential for the sociologist.[18]

Social phenomena arise from the relation and adjustment of the inner and outer systems of reality. While the inner is a complex and coherent system of desires and motivations, the outer is a coherent system of environmental factors and social symbols. When the outer system is utilized as the means, conditions, or opportunity for adjusting the inner, it is termed *environment*. Thus the social sciences investigate the relationships between the inner and outer systems. Since the physical sciences, in contrast, study only the outer order, their subject matter differs fundamentally from that of the social sciences.

The aims and method of both the physical and social sciences are, however, broadly similar, for they seek to determine the "consistency and coherence of reality." As such, argues MacIver, no science is ever "concerned with facts as isolated facts." "No facts ever speak for themselves" and consequently "come into being only with the work of interpretation." Therefore all science requires the scientist to use his inner system of reality to interpret outer reality, or in the social sciences, the special system produced by the interaction of the inner and outer. The researcher thus never deals merely with empirical facts but always with his own interpretation and selection of them. This subjective theory of knowledge resembles the philosophical view that the outside world of noumena can never be known as it is but only as man perceives and conceives it, as phenomena.

Consequently, according to MacIver, sociology differs from the natural and physical sciences not by its aspiration to different goals but by its investigation of distinct data. Its phenomena "involve a kind of causation unknown in the purely physical world, since they are 'motivated,' in fact brought into being, by that elusive and complex, but undeniable reality, the mentality of man." To deal adequately with these phenomena, sociology needs its own special viewpoint. Essential in sociological methods of inquiry is the exercise of creative imagination, logical analysis, and logical synthesis by the investigator.[19] He must select his problem and data; and he must learn to use his insight to achieve an accurate interpretation of the relationships between the inner and outer reality systems. The inescapable subjectivism of the researcher means that complete accuracy and verification are never assured and sociological knowledge is always only approximate.

In brief, since subjective interpretation is the only method for understanding human motivation and desires which enter into all social phenomena, strict objectivism is impossible. By this abstract argument MacIver laid the foundation for a modification of the view that sociologists can approach their data entirely without subjective values, preferences, or biases.

Although usually expressed with greater precision and sophistication by MacIver, these same subjectivist tenets appeared in the writings of other sociologists.[20] For example, Henry P. Fairchild attributed the uniqueness of sociology to its study of "the relations of human beings with their human environment." Willard Waller initiated his explanation of scientific method by indicating how insight and imagination enter into all human perception and permit man to perceive spatial and temporal totalities.[21] The scientific method itself involves the mental act of combining perceived objects in order to attain further insights about interrelationships. In sociology perception of behavior was called "sympathetic penetration," involving interpretation of the imputed purposes and emotions of the actors. Thus all science, particularly the social sciences, are partly an art because the subjective insight of the investigator is always required.

The preceding analysis of the growing concern with scientific method has necessarily been arbitrary in one major respect. The four problems have been discussed as if they were separate and independent; actually they are interrelated and interdependent. Thus sociologists invoked the criteria of empiricism and concreteness to reject the use of subjective data and to defend statistics; they preferred induction to deduction and thereby minimized the role of personal biases and prejudices in sociological investigations; and by stressing multicausational explanations, they encouraged the case method which seeks to interrelate the plurality of factors operative in producing social phenomena. Irrespective of their specific viewpoints on any one of these issues, however, sociologists of the second era were united by a common, underlying purpose: the quest to make sociology more scientific.

Evidence of this shared goal is also found in the actual research and theory in the three general divisions of sociological study: human nature and personality, social structure and community organization, and social change. Since the Middle West completed its seizure of leadership from the East after World War I, and since the most active sociology department in the Midwest developed at the University of Chicago, scientific research and theory in social psychology, social structure, and social change at this university deserve special attention.

Human Nature and Personality: The Chicago School

The major organizational changes within sociology, its reassessment of the sanctions and principles of inquiry, and the developments within American society as a whole all contributed to the rise of social psychology as a distinct area within sociology after World War I. American society was experiencing a general trend toward introspection as evidenced in the increasing popularity of confessional magazines and books, the breakdown of the sex taboo, and a growing concern with emotional problems and mental welfare. Rejecting the earlier, unqualified faith in progress and becoming increasingly aware of the significance of nonrational forces in human behavior, sociologists were led to investigate the realm of man's psychic life. Sociology, they argued, was in need of reliable scientific knowledge about the forces operative in the formation, adjustment, and maladjustment of the human personality. While some research had already been done, much more was needed to establish scientific laws pertaining to human personality. As sociology expanded research dealing with social attitudes, personality development, and personality organization and disorganization multiplied throughout the country, using both statistical and life-history methods. At the University of Chicago this research activity was particularly evident, and the theoretical orientation which came to prevail there has come to be known as *interactionist social psychology*.

The two earliest social psychology texts had been published in 1908, one by the English psychologist William McDougall and the other by the American sociologist, Edward A. Ross. Both books were essentially biologically oriented, attributing human civilization to the nature and quality of inherent human tendencies. Ross was fundamentally concerned with the social control of the biological inclinations of mankind as a whole and of separate human groups which he called *races*. McDougall's more influential volume was the first systematic exposition of human instincts. It presented a set of psychic characteristics as the basic elements in all human behavior, whose transmission might be studied in a manner similar to the Mendelian units of inheritance. Following the physiological orientation of the German psychologist Wilhelm Wundt, McDougall viewed instincts as the basic springs of human thought and action and of the will and character of individuals and nations. When these instincts were developed under the guidance of intellect, man was made more moral and altruistic and civilization improved.

Early in the 1920s this popular theory of instincts as elaborated by McDougall and others came under heavy fire from philosophers, psychologists, and such sociologists as L. L. Bernard and Ellsworth Faris. Revolt against the instinct theories had been on foot for some time when Bernard published his *Instincts: A Study in Social Psychology* (1924). He rested his critique both on the kaleidoscopic state of the classification of instincts and the disregard of environmental factors in explaining personality development. After examining 2000 books by 1700 authors, Bernard enumerated 15,789 separate instincts subsumed under 6,131 types and concluded that the instinct concept had become too inconsistent, uncritical, and inaccurate for scientific use. Furthermore, he demonstrated how a theory of personality development can be established without reference to so-called instincts, many of which are not inherited but the consequence of social environmental forces. These learned behavior forms should be called *habits*, Bernard suggested, and those which are not learned he termed *reflexes*. By careful use of these concepts it is possible to investigate the process whereby the environment modifies the biologically given nature of man into human personalities.

Bernard thus articulated two of the three major prevailing arguments against instinct doctrine. He demonstrated that the classification of instincts lacked scientific precision and clarity and that the presupposition of biological determinism—which conflicted with sociologists' assumption of the psychic nature of social phenomena—was particularistic.

A third criticism based on the scientific prerequisites of concreteness and observability was leveled against the instinct theory by Ellsworth Faris. In his classic article, "Are Instincts Data or Hypotheses?" Faris maintained that no factual basis exists to establish the reality and existence of instincts. He insisted that ethnological data disprove the presence of any constant relationship between given behavior patterns and specified instincts. Members of nonliterate societies frequently either express their "instincts" differently from Western man or possess behavior patterns missing among

Europeans. Thus, he concluded that instincts are merely hypothetical constructs; even if man possesses them at birth, they are so quickly and continuously modified by the culture that they can never be detected in their purity. Consequently Faris urged empirical investigation of the socialization process, that is, the development whereby the child becomes a participating personality in his own society.

With the collapse of the instinct theory, the interactionist social psychology propounded by Charles H. Cooley, John Dewey, George H. Mead, and William I. Thomas gained ascendancy. Since the outstanding proponents of this orientation, except Cooley, were at one time associated with the University of Chicago, their approach has also come to be known as the *Chicago School of Social Psychology.*

According to the social interactionists, biological factors such as the instincts do not play a determining role in the formation and growth of personality. The child is born neither human nor social; at birth he is simply an animal organism belonging to a particular biological species. Ordinarily he is born into a small, face-to-face social group—the family— where he experiences social interaction with parents, siblings, and others, and acquires language, behavior patterns, and familiarity with and acceptance of the values and goals of his society. Along with this indoctrination into the culture of his group, he develops a notion of himself as a self, or ego, which makes him all the more human and social because he now responds directly to the expectations of others and to the internalized moral codes of the group. The child thus becomes self-conscious and plays social roles in accordance with the expectations of others in order to attain their respect and acceptance. As the individual matures he modifies and adjusts his personality developed in childhood by extending the attitudes and values acquired in primary groups to other social situations. This theory of personality development was generally accepted by the members of the Chicago School.

Prior to its elaboration by Cooley, Mead, Thomas, Faris, and others, this theory was expressed in embryonic form in the writings of William James and James M. Baldwin.[22] Baldwin was among the first to overcome the traditional, dualistic mind-body explanation of human behavior. He in turn acknowledged his indebtedness to two sources: first, German idealistic thought with its metaphysical notion that the self is a self-realizing unit in an organic, progressing, spiritual whole; and second, the English school of Darwinian evolution which encouraged the scientific study of the child. By joining these intellectual traditions Baldwin became one of the first psychologists to stress the interrelatedness of biological and social factors in the process of personality development.

A more sociological emphasis was given to Baldwin's theories in the writings of Charles H. Cooley.[23] Having accepted Goethe's notion that "man is a whole, a unity," Cooley opposed all particularisms, especially biological determinism. Life is a whole, and the individual and society are inseparable; they are "twin-born" and "two sides of the same coin." Nor is man part animal and part social. Any human personality is an intricate product of both nature and nurture. The acquisition of speech, for example, demands both organic predisposition and the preexistence of symbolic communication in the group into which man is born. Although he never engaged in carefully planned social psychological research projects himself, Cooley observed human behavior around him—especially the development of his own children—and formulated several sociological concepts which have been exceedingly valuable in subsequent research and generalizations about human behavior.

Being unable to survive without the help of others, Cooley noted, man is almost everywhere found as a member of a family group during his earliest years. Families are characteristically small, face-to-face groups in which associations are intimate and within which members share a common sense of belongingness, a *we-feeling*. As the child develops his social world expands and he participates in play and neighborhood groups which are similarly characterized by face-to-face forms of association. Within these *primary groups*, as Cooley called them, the basic structure of the personality and common human social ideals are established. As a result of the universal existence of similar primary groups, men everywhere possess common attributes called *human nature:* "those sentiments and impulses that are human in being superior to those of lower animals, and also in the sense that they belong to mankind at large, and not to any particular race or time."[24] During man's early years of life within primary groups when he acquires a knowledge of his culture, respect for its values and goals, and the ability to understand and manipulate language, he also develops a conception of himself. This *self*—which Cooley picturesquely termed the "looking-glass self"—is attained when the child becomes able to imagine how he appears to others, how others evaluate his appearance and behavior, and when he himself experiences an emotional reaction to that evaluation. Since the ability to manipulate language symbols is a prerequisite to the acquisition of the self, the notion of "I" is always social in origin.

The social interactionist theory of the development of personality acquired philosophical perspective and depth through the contributions of George Herbert Mead. Following Charles Darwin and Wilhelm Wundt, he maintained a genetic-behavioristic viewpoint and, like Cooley, viewed imitation as an oversimplified explanation of the socialization process. Human social interaction results not merely from copying behavior from others; the process is complex and entails meanings, significant symbols, conversation of gestures, role taking, notions of the "generalized others," and the development of self in terms of an "I" and a "me."

Human behavior, unlike animal behavior, involves social interaction through the use of language: significant symbols whose meanings are learned slowly through a process of gestural and attitudinal "conversation." The meaningfulness of human behavior is acquired in the carrying out of *social acts* in which the actions of one individual serve as a stimulus to a response from another individual. Individuals are thus linked together as reciprocally interacting social objects within a social context. Social acts occur from the time of birth when parents and other persons respond to the infant. People become *social objects* to the child and in contrast to physical objects, which the child learns to notice later, they respond to him and express emotions. However, the child's participation in meaningful social acts must await his development of a self. Since children must learn to imagine the roles of others and thereby to anticipate responses others will make to their own actions, they play at *taking the role of others*, holding conversations with themselves in terms of these other roles. This kind of double-stimulation prepares them to anticipate the social consequences of their own actions. In short, the social act is structured and made meaningful.

Taking the role of others also permits the child to become aware of himself as a social object of action and response to action. Mead called the subjective, acting, unpredictable, and impulsive element of the self the *I* and contrasted it with the objective element of the self, the *me*. As soon as the *I* acts, it is already the object of thought and thus the *me*; moreover, one's notion of the *me* corresponds to internalized group standards and the attitudes others have toward one. When the child has finally learned to imagine not only what separate individuals think of him, but how his actions are evaluated in terms of societal norms, he is responding to one or more *generalized others*. And with the internalization of the generalized others, Mead concluded, the child possesses a conscience.

The third major proponent of the social interactionist orientation was William I. Thomas. As an exponent of empirical research in a research-minded era, he exercised extensive influence on both his colleagues and students investigating problems of personality formation and social behavior.[25] Although Thomas retained a fundamental interest in the problem of social change, he is perhaps best known for his concrete investigations of the multiple factors operative in the formation, organization, and disorganization of personality in different social situations, as for example, in the Polish peasant community, in the American city, and in delinquency areas. His most common technique for the collection of data was the life-history method, and most of his social psychological generalizations are supported by case histories or other personal documents, although he increasingly utilized statistics after his marriage to Dorothy Swaine Thomas. Except in his very earliest writings, he held that personality is the product of human interaction in social settings. While his theory of the process of personality development is nowhere systematically presented, it can be reconstructed from his various writings.

All men, maintained Thomas, possess unique biological structures and temperamental inclinations. Nevertheless, personality is predominantly the product of the interaction of a large number of attitudes which can be grouped into four fundamental *wishes*. These wishes are either personal—the wish for new experience and the wish for security—or social—the wish for response and the wish for recognition. The dynamics and direction of personality development ultimately derive from these wishes and their dialectic interaction.[26]

Since men can satisfy their wishes only as members of social groups, Thomas argued, wishes are manifested in terms of both subjective *attitudes* and corresponding objective *values*.* Personality organization and disorganization are construed as dependent on the relative agreement or disagreement between attitudes and values; and Thomas' types of personalities, such as the "Philistine," the "Bohemian," and the "creative individual," are distinguished in terms of the predominance of certain attitudes and values. Thomas also distinguished between two types of societies: those in

---

* Thomas' *values* are objective in the sense that they are composed of group-shared interests; attitudes may be similar but are never identical.

which the social organization sets a premium on personal wishes and those in which social wishes are especially valued. Correspondingly, these societies are marked by different "runs of attention" or sets of definitions of the situation—the meanings of social situations and the behavior expected of individuals in different contexts. As they are socialized individuals acquire these definitions, integrate them into their personalities, and reflect them in their organization of attitudes. Personality disorganization comes about when the individual is unable to alter these definitions sufficiently to meet the demands for different kinds of behavior in changed social conditions. Consequently, the individual suffers from a lack of satisfaction or undue repression of his basic desires.

The years following World War I were peculiarly well suited for the emergence of a sociological social psychology. Colleges and universities were expanding, research was increasing, and American society was expressing a greater interest in man's nonrational make-up. While pursuing their scientific study of human irrationality sociologists reassessed and rejected the existing instinct approach. Consequently they investigated other orientations. The social interactionist approach developed at the University of Chicago became the most extensively known and the one most commonly employed in research. Although its major proponents explored different aspects of man's psychic life, Cooley, Mead, Thomas, and others agreed that the development of personality took place within social groups through social interaction and the use of language.

Social Structure and Community Organization: Park

Under Robert E. Park's energetic teaching and research, sociology of the community became a second field in which the Chicago Department of Sociology won unrivaled prominence in this period.[27] Park's particular preoccupation with urban theory and research should be viewed in relation to his more comprehensive conception of social structure and change and to his concern with urban social reform then current in the larger society. Indeed, the studies of contemporary American urban social conditions which were undertaken at Chicago seem to have derived their impetus, in large measure, from Park's adroitness in channeling the zeal for urban reform into a disciplined and objective inquiry of urban life.

Park's own earlier background had equipped him with a sympathetic understanding of social reform. Referring to his early career as a newspaper reporter, he once described himself as one of the first and humbler muckrakers. Several years after his journalistic ventures he became secretary of the Congo Reform Association and later a secretary to Booker T. Washington at Tuskegee Institute. As a sociologist, Park certainly did not identify sociology and social reform. But he did assume that the socially useful knowledge which would be supplied by sociology as its scientific function would be applicable to reform. He did not regard the sociologist as committed to the practical application of such knowledge—social technologists have this function.

Park conceived sociology as seeking "natural laws and generalizations in regard to human nature and society, irrespective of time and place."[28] This definition is based on a conception of science drawn from Wilhelm Windelband and Heinrich Rickert, two German methodologists who sharply distinguished science from history. History studies events: the concrete, dated, localized, particular, individual, and unique. Science studies objects —the typical, recurrent, and general—which are defined conceptually and allocated to classes, types, and species so that general conclusions can be derived. Following this view, Park noted that sociology has its own objects of investigation: personalities, groups, institutions, and societies, each with its subclasses, characteristics, and typical modes of change. He believed that generalizations about these objects should be made with the aid of the natural history technique—a kind of composite of the case-study and life-history approaches.

Park's central intellectual concern with the sociological study of the modern city may be explained on four principal grounds: (1) urbanization embodies the problems and processes basic to the evolution of civilization, which is the distinctive realm for sociological inquiry; (2) since the city is the dominant locus of the forces in social change, urban transformations precede broader social changes; (3) the city offers a convenient laboratory for studying the variability of human nature and rapid institutional modifications; (4) the rapidity of change in the city creates "the social problem" and social disorganization, the study of which is practically useful to social agencies engaged in melioristic activity.

In accordance with his conception of scientific procedure, Park viewed the city as an object having its own characteristics and modes of change (or natural history), which, moreover, reflect the general evolution of civilization. His theory of urban society—and of social organization and change in civilized society generally—appears to represent an effort to reconcile the opposing theoretical viewpoints of Comte and Spencer.

Beginning with Spencer's emphasis on the role of the division of labor and competition in initiating social relations, Park postulated the foundation of social stability in the processes of evolution. As one of the biological orders in the "web of nature," man is fundamentally enmeshed in the struggle for existence and competition. Park took an additional cue from the plant and animal ecologists who observed that within the biotic habitat these processes produce a natural order, which is discernible in the territorial distribution of plants and animals and in their interdependency as a natural economy. Following this ecological argument, Park reasoned that competition distributes and organizes the human population spatially into an occupationally differentiated unit within a geographically limited locale. This natural (symbiotic) territorial and occupational arrangement, with an organic unity, is called *community*.

But human association necessarily evokes another level of orderliness definable in terms of Comte's viewpoint and organized around consensus and communication. Man cannot long continue to treat his own kind as mere utilities, as part of the flora and fauna of the natural habitat. Understandings, with intent, design, purpose, and consensus, become manifest as the process of communication erects stable relationships which are customary, conventional, institutional, moral, and cultural. Such relationships result from the efforts of individuals to act collectively. Social relations assume a serial and determinate sequence (succession): economic organization derives from *competition*, though it also acquires a customary ordering; the state and law develop from *conflict;* social organization emerges from *accommodation;* and a characteristic personality type and cultural heritage arise out of *assimilation.* These processes and the social and cultural patterns which they stimulate are termed *society.*

Like all human association, therefore, the city embodies characteristics both of an organism and an artifact, of community and society. The city is the result of competitive and communicative processes.

As a distinctive mode of human settlement and collective existence, the modern city has an ecological (a physical or community) organization which is centered in the market or in exchange relations. The boundaries of the community, set as they are by local geography and the major avenues of transportation, reflect the position of the city as a center of a region of specialized production with a correspondingly widely extended trade area. The ecological pattern within the city reveals the operation of competition both in distributing the population residentially and occupationally and in locating the specialized functions of the division of labor. More specifically, residential, commercial, and industrial competition, and especially the competition between commerce and industry, influence the spatial arrangement of the city.

In the distribution of population and functions, competition initiates several other processes. For example, there is the sifting and sorting of population and functions which accompanies competition that is termed *segregation.* Since the competitive strength of the diverse, segregated social units is unequal, there is *dominance.* This process is evidenced in the differential land values in the urban area.

As a result of the operation of these processes of competition, segregation, and dominance, land-use patterns emerge. Particular localities which have become differentiated and specialized according to residential composition or functional activity are called *natural areas.* They are "natural," Park maintained, because "they are not planned, and because the order they display is not the result of design, but rather a manifestation of tendencies inherent in the urban situation."[29] Just as the city as a whole can be conceptualized as an object and studied scientifically, so each natural area can be investigated in terms of its own characteristics and mode of change.

The concept of natural area became the point of departure for many studies of the Chicago community undertaken by Park and his students. Using physical mobility and land values as indices of competition for space, they described the city as a series of concentric circles, each circumscribing certain natural areas. In addition to land values which assume a typical gradient pattern of distribution, other social phenomena disclose similar manifestations. Thus the suicide rates studied by Ruth Cavan, the divorce and desertion rates investigated by Ernest Mowrer, and the juvenile delinquency rates reported by Clifford Shaw and Henry McKay all reveal typical distributions throughout the several natural areas of Chicago.

Other students of Park investigated specific natural areas or social groups within one or more areas. Norman S. Hayner studied the hotel dweller and Nels Anderson the hobo; Louis Wirth wrote *The Ghetto* (1928), Frederick M. Thrasher *The Gang* (1927), and Harvey W. Zorbaugh *The Gold Coast and the Slum* (1928).

Not only are natural areas distinguished by ecological traits, such as age composition, ethnic make-up, occupational use, social and physical mobility, and land values, but by characteristic cultural phenomena as well. Each natural area tends to become a cultural area with "*its* own peculiar traditions, customs, conventions, standards of decency, and propriety, and, if not a language of its own, at least a *universe of discourse*," in which words and acts have a certain meaning.[30] The origins and meanings of these cultural forms can be found, Park declared, by using the life-history technique to investigate the experiences which contribute to the personality development of individuals in these areas.

Meanings of cultural forms are thus to be sought in the sphere of individual personalities. Accordingly, Park's comments about communication, convention, consensus, and moral order, which are characteristic of cultural areas, attest the cruciality of *individual* intent, will, and design in meanings. Orderliness on the cultural level is volitional and individualistic. And "social relations are finally and fundamentally personal relations" governed by attitudes and wishes. Since only attitudes (tendencies to act) are objectively revealed—are expressive and communicable—they represent the elementary social forces. However, attitudes are means for expressing the psychologically more basic wishes for security, new experience, response, and recognition, as proposed by W. I. Thomas. Thus the attitudes and wishes of the individual become fundamental both to social orderliness and social change.

In this perspective urban social structure is a constellation of individuals each of whom occupies a definite position with reference to the others. Their relations are not defined by mere physical distance; they are rather a matter of *social distance*, the attitudinal "tendency to approach, but not too near."[31] Social distance can be gauged as gradations of understanding and intimacy, which tend to place each member of a group or community in relation to all others.* This position, or *social status*, of each person reflects a consensus of attitudes and judgments of others and, as such, is conditioned by conformity with the standards of the group or community and by participation in its activities.

The concepts of social distance and social status were employed by Park and his students to analyze the processes by which divergent racial and ethnic groups are incorporated into urban society. Although Park's interest in the "race problem" appears at times to bulk so large as to be independent of other concerns, it is, nevertheless, a part of his general conception of change brought on by the city. Park's viewpoint extensively influenced much of the research of sociologists in the developing field of ethnic and race relations in the 1920s and 1930s.[32]

Park's account of the natural history of ethnic and race relations is based on his larger theory of ecology, social processes, social distance, attitudes and wishes.[33] His theory of race relations, which assume the pattern of a cycle of contact, competition, conflict, accommodation, and assimilation, incorporates the following views:

1. The problem of "race relations" is essentially the problem of race-conscious peoples who generally treat one another as representatives of

---

* The conception of social distance was developed and applied in research by E. S. Bogardus and subsequently used by various sociologists and social psychologists, especially in the study of ethnic relationships.

stereotyped group categories rather than as individuals. Interracial intimacies and understanding tend to be prohibited.

2. Race-consciousness develops in large part because economic competition within an ecological order can easily be changed into conflict. The physical visibility of some characteristics of racial groups, especially skin color, makes competitors conscious of one another and provokes antagonism. Eventually, patterns of social distance are established.

3. Whenever conventional symbols of distance—indicative of the accommodation of initial group conflict—are not observed, "race prejudice" is aroused. Attempts to modify the subordinate status of a racial group necessarily elicit prejudice because violation of accepted symbols of inferiority seem to threaten the superior group by changing established lines of social distance.

4. Any disintegration of *caste* distinctions, which function to maintain social distance, stimulates such race prejudice. Since caste relations are often maintained, in part, and made workable by an interpersonal etiquette guaranteeing the persistence of social distance between races, any non-observance of etiquette tends to bring a crumbling of caste distinctions and established social distance.

5. Maintenance of social distance between racial groups, however, is rarely completely successful because miscegenation and assimilation occur. These processes tend to develop a distinctive personality type—the *marginal man*—who may be either a biological or a cultural hybrid or both. Marginal individuals are generally refused membership in the superior group to which they aspire; they are often rejected by the subordinate group as well. Since they experience divided loyalties and frustrations in their social aspirations, marginal men manifest characteristic personality conflicts. This analysis by Park stimulated other sociological studies of marginal personalities, the best known of which is Everett V. Stonequist's *Marginal Man* (1937).

No matter how important such special interests as race relations may seem to be to Park, they still assumed a place in his underlying preoccupation with the problems of urban life. His qualitative research, especially the natural- and life-history techniques, and his theory of human ecology and the social processes were means to advance the understanding of urban structure and change.

Social Change: Ogburn

Just as Thomas and Park brought eminence to the University of Chicago Department of Sociology in social psychology and urban sociology, so William F. Ogburn won a similar prominence for the Chicago group in the field of social and cultural change. In 1927 Ogburn came to Chicago from Columbia University, where he had taught for eight years, had first stated his theory of social change, and had earlier received his doctorate under F. H. Giddings. During the twenty-four years of his active academic life at Chicago he was energetic in promoting the use of statistical techniques in sociology. The importance attached to statistics is reflected in his studies of population structure and change, invention and technology, and trends of social change. He was the editor and co-author of the influential *Recent*

Social Trends (1933). This inquiry, as well as others in the field of social change, emphasizes the culture lag thesis, the first formulation of which was published in his *Social Change* (1922). Despite numerous criticisms this theory has remained an accepted, if not a dominant, interpretation of social and cultural change in American sociology.[34]

The culture lag theory, which proposes that material culture changes more rapidly than nonmaterial culture so that a lag is created between the two realms, shares certain assumptions with the prevailing western European interpretation of change. It assumes that culture is an organic unity and that change moves in a straight-line or rectilinear direction. Ogburn's lag thesis thus continues certain ideas which were used by Comte and by early American sociologists.

The lag theory assumes a conception of culture as an organic whole, with its parts harmoniously integrated, which derives from a similar notion of society found in the classical Greek, the Augustinian Christian, and early modern progress notions of change. Ogburn's division of culture into a material sphere of objective artifacts and a nonmaterial sphere of patterned ideas, ideals, and behavior does not contradict this insistence on the harmonious, integrated interdependency of the parts of culture. Indeed, Ogburn actually compares culture to an organism with all of its parts interlinked and interdependent. By implication, these parts have a logically necessary and limited—rather than a historically accidental—relationship to one another.[35]

The lag theory also adheres to the view that change moves in a constant, linear direction. It resembles the older Augustinian Christian and early modern progress versions of change which, associated as they were with organic conceptions of society, also assumed social and culture change to involve linear direction. In the Augustinian Christian version, change was providentially directed and in the early modern progress version, the natural laws of progress provided direction. Ogburn's scheme postulates a similar linear direction of culture change, though it derives from continuous technological improvement. Because of "the tendency of a superior tool to replace one that is inferior," he insists that there are universal stages of material (or technological-economic) culture which involve a fairly reliable temporal sequence. Accordingly, his position resembles the unilinear stages theory of social evolution. However, Ogburn recognizes that diffusion negates any possibility of a determinate sequence of natural stages in the development of given social institutions as proposed by the late-nineteenth-century social evolutionists.

For Ogburn, progress in tool-making gives culture change a linear direction in time because change is a cumulative process. Culture accumulates as each generation adds to the legacy left by the preceding one. These cumulative additions of successive generations may result from invention (internal to the culture) or from diffusion (external to it). The more knowledge accumulates, the more inventions are possible. Therefore, culture changes may be said to accumulate (since there are so few losses) at an exponential rate—like compound interest—through time.

Most immediately, inventions depend on the existent state of the culture base (or prior cultural preparation, out of which they must arise) and on the social values or valuations which tend to create a demand for innovation. These two factors are more important than the mental ability of the population.

Acceptance of inventions may be resisted if the invention does not seem to operate efficiently at first, if it disturbs other sectors of the culture, if there are survivals which serve the same purpose, if economic costs are excessive, or if there is ignorance. Habit and hostile attitudes (fear of the new, devotion to things as they are, reverence for the past) and vested interests, may also deter acceptance of the invention.

While Ogburn concedes that inventions can originate in either the nonmaterial or material culture, he is, however, committed to the view that inventions in the modern world occur more frequently and more rapidly in the material-technological sphere. He actually favors "the hypothesis of the greater importance of the sequence of technology causing social changes" rather than of social changes stimulating mechanical inventions because "it appears easier to find illustrations of technology causing changes in social conditions."[36] This viewpoint is consistent with his argument that material culture has a logical or instrumental priority over the nonmaterial, whether there is a temporal priority or not.

The consequent differential rate of change in the two spheres of modern culture is expressed as a *lag*. Since culture is assumed to be an organic, interdependent unity of parts, a strain is developed between the more rapidly changing (or "leading") technological-material culture and the related, though less rapidly changing or responding (or "lagging"), nonmaterial culture.

Ogburn contends that eventually a more harmonious adjustment of the invention and its related cultural parts will occur. Just how adjustment can be objectively ascertained—free from value judgments—is difficult to prove. He confesses that one's notion of adaptation may depend on attitudes toward life, progress, and religious beliefs.

In the various sectors of the nonmaterial culture, there is unequal responsiveness in adjusting to the changes which are initiated by the inventions of science and technology. The economy adjusts most readily; government, family, education, philosophy, religion, follow with art as the least responsive or most resistant.

By virtue of its conception of varying institutional responsiveness to adjustment, the culture lag scheme is thus readily applicable to the explanation of the sources and solution of certain social problems and forms of social and personality disorganization. Total social reconstruction can be attempted by acceleration of the rate of change in the several social institutions (the dependent variables), by deceleration of the rate of change in science and technology (the independent variable), or by both procedures. Yet Ogburn claims that social and personal disorganization can also be mitigated by more minor, less basic, alterations in the structure of the society.

Particularly applicable to a society in which technology, science, and industrialization play a dominant role, the culture lag doctrine has been adopted as an explanation of social maladjustments by Harry E. Barnes, Abbott P. Herman, Mabel A. Elliott, and Francis E. Merrill, and more recently—though with modifications—by Herbert A. Bloch. The lag thesis persists in contemporary theoretical developments in sociology as is indicated by its incorporation in the interpretation of social change in Parsons' theory of the social system. Nevertheless, the lag doctrine, which was used in many concrete empirical investigations of technological change during the years 1925–1935, is more prominently featured in the second than in either of the other periods.

Viewing the second period of American sociology as a whole, it appears to have been as preoccupied with making the discipline scientific as the earlier period was devoted to ameliorating social conditions and accelerating progress. Scientific method became the crucial, if not the central, concern of the years 1920 to 1935. Principles of inquiry were examined critically and were refined in the course of their application to research problems.

As the intermediate period in the history of the discipline, the sociology of 1918 to 1935 manifests relationships with both formative and contemporary eras. It reflects certain continuities with the earlier period. For instance, sociologists between World War I and the Depression sought to explain how the irrational social forces of human nature develop and operate, how urban living structures social relations and influences social behavior; and how technological inventions produce social change and strain the interrelationships within the total society. The second period also anticipated certain developments of the most recent era. The professional expansion after World War I permitted the specialization of subfields and research techniques during the 1920s and facilitated their further elaboration in more recent years. The achievement of scientific respectability of the discipline in the second period laid the basis for increasing interdisciplinary ventures and made possible subsequent acknowledgment of utilitarian inclinations without relinquishing scientific objectivity and returning to the bias of a belief in progress. And, finally, the promotion of empirical research contributed to the formulation of theories, elements of which have recently been incorporated into systematic sociological theory.

Footnotes to Chapter Two

1. Meroney, W. P.: "The Membership and Program of Twenty-five Years of the American Sociological Society," *Publications of the American Sociological Society* **XXV**:55–68 (May, 1931).

2. For a present-day symposium along similar lines, though primarily devoted to three social sciences, see John Gillin (Ed.): *For a Science of Social Man: Convergences in Anthropology, Sociology, and Psychology*, New York, The Macmillan Co., 1954.

3. Groves, Ernest H.: "Science and Social Unrest," *Scientific Monthly* **10**:157–158 (February, 1920).

4. Weatherly, Ulysses G.: "Racial Pessimism," *Publications of the American Sociological Society* **XVIII**:1–17 (1924).

5. Small, Albion W.: "The Future of Sociology," *Publications of the American Sociological Society* **XV**:174–193 (1921).

6. Ogburn, William F.: "The Historical Method in the Analysis of Social Phenomena," *Publications of the American Sociological Society* **XVI**:70–83 (1922).

7. Bernard, Luther L.: "Scientific Method and Social Progress," *American Journal of Sociology* 31:1–18 (July, 1925).

8. Faris, Ellsworth: "Are Instincts Data or Hypotheses?," *American Journal of Sociology* 27:184–196 (September, 1921); and Faris, Ellsworth: "Ethnological Light on Psychological Problems," *Publications of the American Sociological Society* XVI:113–120 (1922).

9. North, Cecil C.: *Social Differentiation*, Chapel Hill, University of North Carolina Press, 1926.

10. Hayes, Edward C.: "The Sociological Point of View," *Publications of the American Sociological Society* XVI:1–16 (1922).

11. See especially Lundberg, George A., Read Bain, and Nels Anderson: *Trends in American Sociology*, New York, Harper & Brothers, 1929.

12. Bain, Read: "An Attitude on Attitude Research," *Publications of the American Sociological Society* XXII:186 (1928); and Young, Kimball: "The Measurement of Personal and Social Traits," *Publications of the American Sociological Society* XXI:92–105 (1927).

13. Ogburn, William F.: "Bias, Psycho-Analysis, and the Subjective in Relation to the Social Sciences," *Publications of the American Sociological Society* XVII:62–74 (1923).

14. Rice, Stuart A.: "What is Sociology?," *Social Forces* 10:319–326 (March, 1932).

15. Fairchild, Henry Pratt: "The Possibility, Character, and Function of an Applied Sociology," *Social Forces* 11:182–187 (December, 1932).

16. Ellwood, Charles A.: "The Uses and Limitations of Behaviorism in Sociology," *Publications of the American Sociological Society* XXIV:74–82 (1929); Ellwood, Charles A.: "Scientific Method in Sociology," *Social Forces* 10:15–21 (October, 1931); and *Social Forces* 11:44–50 (October, 1932); Ellwood, Charles A.: *Methods in Sociology*, Durham, N. C., Duke University Press, 1933.

17. MacIver, Robert M.: "Is Sociology a Natural Science?," *Publications of the American Sociological Society* XXV:25–35 (1930); MacIver, Robert M.: "Social Causation," *Publications of the American Sociological Society* XXVI:28–36 (1931).

18. The arguments expressed in the two articles here referred to anticipate the subsequent, more extensive, exposition of MacIver's position in his *Social Causation*, Boston, Ginn & Company, 1942.

19. MacIver later referred to this sociological method as "sympathetic reconstruction." See especially his *Social Causation*, Boston, Ginn & Company, 1942, p. 391. For a further discussion of MacIver's theories see the section, Social Action Theory, in Chapter Three.

20. Fairchild, *op. cit.*; Waller, Willard: "Insight and Scientific Method," *American Journal of Sociology* 40:285–297 (November, 1934), and Rice, *op. cit.*

21. Stuart A. Rice, *op. cit.*, also insists that perception is selective and that man is never able to view reality in its entirety but only in part.

22. See especially Baldwin, J. M.: *Ethical Interpretations in Mental Development*, New York, The Macmillan Co., 1913, which influenced Charles H. Cooley, as illustrated in his *Human Nature and the Social Order*, revised, New York, Charles Scribner's Sons, 1922, p. 125. For a general development of this school of social psychology and its basic tenets see Karpf, Fay B.: *American Social Psychology*, New York, McGraw-Hill Book Co., Inc., 1932, Chaps. VI, VII.

23. There is some difficulty in placing Cooley accurately in the development of American sociology. On purely chronological grounds, Cooley is a transitional figure. The publication dates of his three major works: *Human Nature and the Social Order*, New York, Charles Scribner's Sons, 1902, revised, 1922; *Social Organization*, New York, Charles Scribner's Sons, 1909; and *The Social Process*, New York, Charles Scribner's Sons, 1918 place him at the end of the formative era and at the beginning of the second period of American sociology. Moreover, Cooley held the presidency of the American Sociological Society in the transitional year, 1918. According to his social psychological writings, however, he is most appropriately located in the second era because his theories received their widest acclaim after World War I and because they are today accepted as part of the social psychological movement of the 1920s.

    See also, Karpf, *op. cit.*, pp. 291–307; Jandy, Edward C.: *Charles Horton Cooley: His Life and His Social Theory*, New York, The Dryden Press, Inc., 1942; and Odum, Howard W.: *American Sociology*, New York, Longmans, Green and Co., Inc., 1951, p. 109. Odum insists that Cooley is not a member of the first era of American sociology. Instead he associates Cooley with the years 1914 to 1918 which comprise the second period of American sociology according to Odum's scheme.

24. Cooley, Charles Horton: *Social Organization*, New York, Charles Scribner's Sons, 1909, p. 28.

25. See for instance Young, Kimball (Ed.): *Social Attitudes*, New York, Henry Holt & Co., Inc., 1931, a volume comprised of articles by men who openly acknowledged their indebtedness to Thomas.

26. For a detailed analysis of the persistence with which Thomas maintained this theory of the dynamics of personality see Hinkle, Gisela J.: "The 'Four Wishes' in Thomas' Theory of Social Change," *Social Research* 19:464–484 (December, 1952).

27. Park's papers on the community have recently been published. See Park, Robert F.: *Human Communities: The City and Human Ecology*, Glencoe, Ill., The Free Press, 1952.

28. Park, Robert E., and Ernest W. Burgess: *Introduction to the Science of Sociology*, Chicago, University of Chicago Press, 1924, p. 11.

29. Park, Robert Ezra: *Human Communities: The City and Human Ecology*, Glencoe, Ill., The Free Press, 1952, p. 196.

30. *Ibid.*, p. 201.

31. Park and Burgess, *op. cit.*, p. 440.

32. Among them are Romanzo Adams, W. O. Brown, Bertram W. Doyle, E. Franklin Frazier, Charles S. Johnson, A. W. Lind, Donald Pierson, E. B. Reuter, E. V. Stonequist, and Edgar T. Thompson.

33. Park's papers on "race" and ethnic relations have recently been published in *Race and Culture*, Glencoe, Ill., The Free Press, 1950.

34. For a recent critique of the culture lag doctrine see MacIver, R. M., and C. H. Page: *Society: An Introductory Analysis*, New York, Rinehart & Co., Inc., 1949, Chap. 26. From the mid-1930s to the mid-1940s, the lag thesis was subjected to extensive examination—and often criticism—in the sociological journals by Michael Choukas, Hornell Hart, John Mueller, Joseph Schneider, Wilson Wallis, and James Woodard. Joseph Schneider has made a detailed historical analysis of the intellectual antecedents of culture lag theory in an unpublished study.

35. This view is supported by Ogburn's use of the older comparative method

in his account of human culture history. He reconstructed Cro-Magnon Magdalenian nonmaterial culture, which has been irretrievably lost, by inferring it from Eskimo culture, since modern Eskimo and prehistoric Magdalenian material cultures are similar. The comparative method can be used only on the assumption that culture at any stage is an interrelated and interdependent whole. See Ogburn, William F., and Meyer F. Nimkoff: *Sociology*, New York, Houghton Mifflin Co., 1946, p. 33.

36. Ogburn and Nimkoff: *op. cit.*, p. 865.

chapter three

Reciprocity of Theory, Research, and Application (1935—1954)

The great Depression and World War II have had a major role in shaping contemporary American sociology. In general, they led many sociologists to shift attention from the task of making sociology scientific to efforts to make the discipline socially useful. In particular, these two pervasive crises influenced sociologists' participation in their professional societies, and affected the principal sources of employment, the dominant fields of sociological interest, the organization, scope, and approach to social research, intellectual sanctions, and even the theoretical developments in American sociology during the last two decades.

Changing Professional Participation, Employment, and Interests

Membership in the American Sociological Society has been subject to extreme fluctuations in numbers within the last two decades. From its earlier peak of 1,567 members in 1932, membership declined to the low point of 997 in 1939. The 1,651 members in 1946 were the result of a slow increase during the war years. But thereafter additions accrued so rapidly that by 1953 the membership totaled 4,027.

During the years of the two great crises sociologists were frequently employed by the Federal government. Throughout the depression years sociologists joined the staffs of the Works Progress Administration, the Department of Agriculture, the TVA, the National Resources Committee, and other federal, state, and local agencies concerned with practical problems of social welfare. With the war, sociologists accepted commissions in the armed forces, participated in training programs for servicemen, became consultants or regular personnel for OSS, OPA, the Department of State, and other federal agencies. Their professional counsel is still employed in the formation of domestic and foreign governmental policy today.

Concurrently, sociological literature and research indicate that sociologists' interests were changing. The tendency for large numbers of sociologists to forego social meliorism in the 1920s and the inclination of social work to separate itself from sociology as an independent academic department with its own professionally trained personnel during the early years of this period helped to bring about a decline of interest in social work. For a time the field of social pathology also diminished in importance, though the founding of the Society for the Study of Social Problems in

1952 suggests a renewed concern with this area. Although social psychology still remains one of the major fields, it no longer holds as preeminent a position as it formerly did. Many younger sociologists are devoting their energies to the more established areas of urban sociology, social institutions, the sociology of family and marriage, social psychiatry, and sociological theory, and to the newer fields of social stratification, industrial sociology, cultural sociology and anthropology, communications and public opinion, medical sociology, aging and retirement, and small group analysis. These trends to some extent reflect a concern with the interactive processes and institutional structure of mass society. The small group has increasingly become the unit of investigation partly because it is often argued that prediction and control of changes in the segments or in the whole of mass society may be possible through extrapolation from small group analysis. Whatever the interests, their pursuit is justified by their contribution to the development of sociology itself.

New Journals, Regional Associations, and Specialized Societies

The establishment of new journals, regional associations, and specialized societies, although not directly related to the two national crises, reflect this expanding range of interests and professional specialization. In 1936 the *American Sociological Review,* a journal issued six times yearly, replaced the *Publications of the American Sociological Society,* which had been the official medium for the annual publication of papers, reports, discussions, and shop talk presented at the yearly meetings of the Society. At the same time E. W. Burgess became editor of the *American Journal of Sociology.* With the appearance of a new journal, *Sociometry,* in 1938, further opportunity was provided for publishing interpersonal and small group research. In 1953 revived interest in social disorganization was signaled by the establishment of the periodical *Social Problems.* Smaller regional publications were also founded during the last two decades, and in at least two instances journals with a national audience, *Social Forces* and *Sociology and Social Research,* became publication media for regional sociological societies.

In 1925 the organization of the first large regional association, the Ohio Valley Sociological Society, set a precedent followed in the 1930s by other regional groups: the Pacific Sociological Society was established in 1930; the Eastern Society in 1935; the Southern in 1936; the Michigan, the Midwestern, and the Southwestern Societies in 1937. Having a combined membership exceeding that of the national society, these regional associations permit greater personal contact, fellowship, and intellectual discussion among groups of professionals than is possible at the national meetings, as well as increased opportunities—particularly for younger sociologists—to present research reports.

Of the numerous new special interest societies the Population Association, founded in 1932, was one of the earliest. The Rural Sociological Society was organized in 1937, with its own journal, *Rural Sociology.* Sociologists and other professionals interested in problems of family life have been active in the National Conference on Family Relations, which was established in 1938. In the same year the American Catholic Sociological Society and its official journal, the *American Catholic Sociological Review*, were founded.

These developments emphasize the increasing division of professional labor in sociology itself. At the same time sociologists were actively participating in cross-disciplinary ventures with other social scientists, especially in their research activities.

Interdisciplinary Research and Academic Integration

The two national emergencies of the period and the increasingly mass character of American society raised problems exceeding the capacities of a single investigator and contributed to new departures in the organization, scope, and approach of social research. Of the large-scale research endeavors requiring cooperative effort and an interdisciplinary social science approach, three are especially notable.

The two-volume *Recent Social Trends* (1933), which involves research undertaken at the request of President Hoover in 1929 and directed by William F. Ogburn and Howard W. Odum, sought to explore the extent and direction of changes in various facets of American society. Using quantitative data wherever possible, these volumes and the related series of monographs based on this larger study report trends in technology, the economy, population structure, family life, recreation, urbanization, education, and other areas of American life. For many years *Recent Social Trends* was a standard reference work for government agencies and social science teachers alike. It remains a landmark in social investigation.

In 1937 Carnegie Corporation provided funds for a comprehensive study of Negro-White relations in the United States. This investigation was directed by Gunnar Myrdal, a Swedish political economist, and was later published as *An American Dilemma* (1944). Although the final integration of the study was the director's own responsibility, the cooperative nature of the basic research is indicated by the work of fifty-one social science advisors in the formulation of the research outline, a seven-member regular staff, thirty-one specialists who prepared separate monographs, and thirty-six staff assistants. *An American Dilemma* compiles a vast amount of historical, economic, political, sociological, and psychological data on Negroes and their relations with non-Negroes in this country. The volume is integrated by Myrdal's interpretation and supplemented by his analysis of the interconnections between science and social values. In its condensed version the work has become a standard textbook in American colleges. The original volumes are still the most comprehensive source of information on Negro-White relations in the United States.

The American Soldier (1949) is a summary of research dealing primarily with the attitudes of military personnel at home and abroad during World War II. Again, the several studies are the collaborative product of a number of social scientists as well as the military and civilian personnel associated with the Research Branch of the Information and Education Division of the War Department. This wartime research has certain continuities with *An American Dilemma* in directorship and financial support. Samuel A. Stouffer, who was in charge of the completion of the earlier study when the war forced Myrdal's return to Sweden, was also the staff director and major author of *The American Soldier*. Funds for publication also came from the Carnegie Corporation, operating through the Social Science Research Council. Many sociologists acclaim *The American Soldier* for advancing empirical research techniques in the field of attitude study; it is commended by others for its theoretical contributions.

This trend of interdisciplinary research was accompanied by several academic innovations in departmental integration and cross-departmental faculty appointments. The Institute of Human Relations at Yale University, founded in 1929 with funds supplied by the Rockefeller Foundation, joins medicine, law, and the social sciences in furthering the study of man. The Institute's researches, especially in the areas of child development, social and cultural aspects of psychiatric problems, and the interdisciplinary study of alcoholism are evidenced by a series of publications. In 1946 Harvard University established the Department of Social Relations under the direction of Talcott Parsons, with a staff comprised of sociologists, cultural anthropologists, and psychologists who collaborate in interdisciplinary studies. *Toward a General Theory of Action* (1951), of which Parsons is the senior author and to which Stouffer again is a contributor, aims at a unified social science theory and was written by representatives of the three disciplines incorporated in this department. The University of North Carolina has an Institute of Research in Social Science and an interdisciplinary faculty seminar under John Gillin's direction concerned with the development of the fundamentals of a behavioristic social science. Another approach to social science cooperation on both the teaching and research levels is represented by the University of Chicago's Committee on Human Development. Finally, the many interdepartmental programs and courses in the social sciences at the undergraduate level are further evidence of this interdisciplinary trend.

Funds for these large-scale integrative projects have come primarily from private foundations and Federal governmental agencies. In 1953 sociologists reported a total of 253 research projects supported by such non-university organizations to the extent of over a million dollars.

Utilitarian Justifications of Sociology

Of all the consequences of the great Depression and World War II, none was more crucial for sociology than the change in intellectual sanctions and goals of the discipline. As the number of sociologists participating in governmental and other public agencies increased, members of the discipline reexamined the question of the relation of values to scientific sociology and began to justify the field on utilitarian grounds. In the previous period the quest for an objective science had led many sociologists to reject the doctrine of progress and to disavow reform. The promotion of human welfare and the discovery of scientific laws about social life had become separate and, in the view of many persons in the discipline, antithetical endeavors. The demand for objectivity, which accompanied the preoccupation with making the field scientific, had frequently come to mean exclusion of concern with values. While sociologists of the second era assumed the ultimate usefulness of sociological knowledge, many of them avoided direct participation in action programs because they did not wish to become identified with specific value preferences. Subsequent extensive involvement of sociologists in these practical programs, especially in the government, led to a scrutiny of the arguments about the relation of the discipline to values and value judgments.

This reconsideration resulted in at least four distinguishable viewpoints, though they overlapped in the specific statements appearing in the journals and elsewhere. First, some humanitarian-minded sociologists contended that, since the Depression revealed a failure of human rather than technological factors, sociologists had a special responsibility to make their knowledge available and useful in social rehabilitation. Robert S. Lynd's widely read *Knowledge for What?* (1939) proclaims this position. Second, others argued that the socially-conditioned character of values justified research into their origins, cultural variability, and mutual interactions. Proponents of this view insisted that such studies could be pursued without violating objectivity. A third argument declared that the attempt to be "value-free" in order to preserve scientific objectivity is unrealistic, if not impossible. As creatures of their culture, sociologists cannot escape altogether its biases and values (some of which are the values upon which modern science rests). Indeed, the very formulation of a problem in social science implies some kind of evaluation. Therefore objectivity can be achieved more adequately, it was claimed, if the researcher becomes conscious of and explicitly specifies his values. His conclusions can then be judged accordingly. This position was presented clearly and convincingly by Gunnar Myrdal in the Appendices of *An American Dilemma*. Finally, scientific method and scientific knowledge were said to be effective means for attaining *any* end; science, including sociology, can be used to achieve humanitarian, democratic, manipulative, exploitative, or totalitarian ends. Determining how science will be used is not part of the scientific role of the sociologist, though in his role as a citizen he may legitimately be concerned with the application of science. George A. Lundberg has been a vigorous protagonist of this position.

From the discussion of the relation of values and sociology, as stimulated by the participation of sociologists in government and other organizations oriented toward practical ends, has come a new intellectual justification of sociology. Although the arguments about the relationship of sociology and values sometimes stand in direct opposition, they ultimately share a fundamental utilitarianism.

A New Function for Sociological Theory

As sociologists came to justify their research on more utilitarian grounds and became more aware of the part values play in prompting scientific inquiry their conceptions of the relationship of theory and research changed significantly. Earlier theory had been so intimately linked with the doctrine of progress, social evolution, and philosophies of history, that many sociologists of the second period were inclined to consider theory as an expression of personal bias and value judgments and, therefore, as inimical to the objectivity required in science. But the painstakingly descriptive data collected in the 1920s proved to be inadequate to meet the demands of the Depression crisis. Recognizing this predicament, many sociologists reconsidered their orientation and attempted to make sociology more useful by employing theory or theories to organize and to interrelate the mass of discrete studies. Moreover, some sociologists welcomed this more favorable attitude toward theory, especially the increasing acceptance of logical systems used to order, articulate, and accumulate research, as a major advance in scientific sociology. Two movements in the late 1930s attest this changing viewpoint. The one sought to integrate existing sociological concepts, and the other to construct systematic theoretical systems. Both the intellectual traditions of *positivism* and of *social action* (not to be confused with organized action for purposes of social reform) were used to build systematic theories. In recent years social action theory has become particularly prominent.

Theory construction thus appropriately became a scientific guide in the social engineering required by the national crises. Since sociologists argue that "facts do not speak for themselves" but require interpretation, they now generally regard the construction of theory or of conceptual models as indispensable to human engineering projects. In this utilitarian era, therefore, "sound theory becomes essentially the most practical thing in the whole scientific realm."[1]

At the same time that systematic theory became a more conspicuous topic in American sociological literature, numerous translations of foreign theoretical treatises were published. According to the writers' enumeration, which sought to be exhaustive, only twelve books in general theory were published between 1915 and 1935, whereas twenty-seven appeared between 1936 and 1953. Similarly, only six translations of foreign theoretical works appeared between 1915 and 1935, whereas from 1936 to 1953 thirteen such books were published. Theories of Continental scholars were thus more readily available to American sociologists.

The Continental impact on American sociological theory was aided, moreover, by the European political upheavals during the 1930s and 1940s. Forced to emigrate, many scholars came to the United States and joined American academic institutions. Having been trained in the Continental traditions of system-building and abstract philosophical thought, they reinforced the theoretical efforts already in progress in the United States.

European Influences

Recent European influences on American theory are consequently very pronounced. Among a number of works,* those of the following four theorists are especially significant for American sociology: Vilfredo Pareto (1848–1923), an Italian economist; Émile Durkheim (1858–1917), a French sociologist; Sigmund Freud (1856–1934), an Austrian psychiatrist and founder of psychoanalysis; and Max Weber (1864–1920), a German historian, political economist, and sociologist.

---

* For example, the writings of Georg Simmel and Karl Mannheim, as well as those of Karl Marx. These have been influential to some small extent in this country, but much less so than the views of Pareto, Durkheim, Freud, and Weber.

Pareto

In American intellectual circles of the 1930s Pareto's sociological writings aroused frequent comment. Their importance for American sociological theory rests primarily on Pareto's conception of the *social system*, his tenet that such a system is in equilibrium, his emphasis on the role of non-rationality in human behavior, and his theory of the circulation of the elite.[2]

In order to make sociology a science of society in spite of the peculiarly variable nature of social phenomena Pareto recommends the *logico-experimental* method as an appropriate investigative procedure. This method embodies two major prerequisites of science: use of logical reasoning and observation of fact without evaluative bias. By applying this procedure to a study of society, Pareto believes that it is possible to determine universal, stable social factors and to formulate them as theoretical concepts. Since Pareto assumes that these stable social elements are in mutual dependency, he conceives society as a social system in a state of equilibrium which tends to be reestablished in spite of modifications (induced by internal or external events) producing temporary or permanent change. The concepts for describing society are themselves part of a logically closed system of interrelated and interdependent variables.

These concepts, reflecting the nature of society, ultimately depend on the character of the actions of the component individuals. Pareto maintains that individuals' actions are for the most part nonlogical; they are not based on rational considerations of means and ends. The determining and constant elements in nonlogical behavior are *residues*, or manifestations of sentiments, which are not expressed directly but only indirectly in terms of widely varying *derivations*.* Pareto sets forth a detailed classification of both the underlying forces in human conduct—the residues—and the rationalizations or cultural forms in terms of which they are expressed—the derivations. He utilizes his concepts of residues and derivations to explain social classes, social institutions, professional groups, and other social phenomena.

His theory of the circulation of the elite posits that the social classes of the society possess the different residues in varying proportions. Thus the governing elite is always strongly motivated by the residues of "combination" and of the "persistence of aggregates." Yet its position of dominance is secure only so long as it remains willing to use physical force in addition to its manipulation of the masses by appeals to their sentiments and residues. Once the elite loses its ability or willingness to use force, and some-

---

* There are six classes of *residues*: I. residues of combination which account for the combining of ideas and things; II. residues of the persistence of aggregates which account for the adherence to tradition; III. residues of the manifestations of sentiments through overt acts; IV. residues in regard to sociability which make for social conformity; V. residues of the integrity of the individual which make man resist social changes in which he is ego-involved; and VI. sexual residues.

There are four classes of *derivations*: I. affirmations which are statements not based on experience; II. references to authorities which may or may not be empirically sound; III. accord with sentiment or principles, or reference to general consensus; and IV. verbal proofs.

times also its superior innovating ability, it is overthrown by new leaders. These new rulers who arise from the masses attain powerful positions in society because they do not hesitate to use physical force to attain their ends. That this cycle of change occurs frequently is amply evidenced in the pages of history, for "history is a graveyard of aristocracies."

Durkheim

Though his books were read by numerous American sociologists for many years, Durkheim's ideas were accorded only limited acceptance primarily because they are inconsistent with certain fundamental assumptions of American sociology.[3] The data of sociology, insists Durkheim, are social facts which must be studied as "things" external to and constraining upon the individual. Explanations of social facts involve other social facts and never conditions or facts belonging to lower evolutionary orders such as psychology or biology. Indeed, society itself is a social fact, an entity *sui generis,* something real in itself and unlike a mere sum of the individuals of which it is composed. But most American sociologists have been unwilling to accept this Durkheimian tenet of society as separate and real in itself because their characteristic voluntaristic nominalism has led them to consider society as the sum of individuals in interaction.

Nevertheless, Durkheim's views on social change, his concept of *anomie* (or normlessness), his theory of the categories of thought, and his sociology of religion have become influential. Reflecting the intellectual tenor of his time, Durkheim cast his theories in the context of social evolution. He maintained that societies typically change from a primitive, homogeneous social life marked by *mechanical solidarity*—a unity based on community of ideas, sentiments, and tradition—to industrial, civilized existence with a highly differentiated division of labor, extensive personality variation, and a predominance of contractual relations characterized by *organic solidarity* —a unity based on functional interdependence and sacredness of the individual. Although it undergoes modifications, social solidarity is always the source of social order because it corresponds to the institutionalized norms which constrain individual behavior.

The process of change tends to develop situations in which the old norms no longer restrain individual behavior and new norms are either absent or unacceptable. Such *anomie,* or normlessness, frequently occurs in the development of urban society, giving rise to personal disorganization and a specific type of suicide which Durkheim calls *anomic suicide.*[4]

Although Durkheim's theory of the categories of thought is formulated as a critique of the nonempirical, a priori mental categories proposed by Immanuel Kant, it is generally interpreted by American sociologists as a contribution to the sociology of knowledge. According to Durkheim, these categories are not innately given. They are developed through human association prevailing at various evolutionary stages of social existence. Such concepts as time, space, force, cause, number, and contradiction are called *collective representations* since they result from the interactions of group life. In the course of evolution the categories accumulate and become permanent parts of the cultural tradition even though the originating conditions may not persist.

Durkheim presented a similarly evolutionary explanation of religious life. Largely on the basis of a case study of the Arunta in Australia, he ascribes the evolutionary origins of religious thought and practice to group existence itself. Thus the major function of religion is the maintenance of social solidarity. In all societies the outstanding characteristic of religion is its distinction between the *sacred* and the *profane*. Things sacred are regarded with awe and reverence and are categorically separate from the commonplace, mundane, or profane.

Freud

Throughout most of its development American sociology has accepted some and rejected other aspects of Freud's psychological theories.[5] Although psychoanalysis developed primarily as a medical therapy, it influenced American sociology because it recognizes the essential irrationality of human behavior and posits a deterministic theory of personality development.[6] Recently, systematic sociological theorists have employed Freud's concept of the *superego* to construct a logical link between individual motivation and social prescriptions of behavior.[7]

Originally Freud considered behavior as the result of a dialectic process between *Eros*, which is the instinct to live and be active, manifested as the *libido*, and *Thanatos*, which is the death instinct or wish to return to a lifeless state of inactivity. Subsequently, however, Freud placed less emphasis on the death instinct and explained behavior by the interactions within the tripartite structure of the human psyche. Specifically, the human psyche is a strictly determined mechanism comprised of the *id*, which is an unconscious force seeking sexual satisfaction in accordance with the "pleasure principle"; the *ego*, which emerges from the id and more or less consciously provides satisfactions in conformity with the "reality principle"; and the *superego*, which evolves from the ego, assimilates the moral standards of the society, and becomes an unconscious conscience. As these psychic components develop during the first five years of life their mutual interaction sets the basic framework of personality. Normal personalities then pass through a latency period from the age of five to thirteen and a pubertal period from the age of thirteen to nineteen, before attaining adulthood. As the personality evolves it maintains an equilibrium among the conflicting id, ego, and superego by the operation of numerous behavior mechanisms. The ones best known and most often utilized by sociologists are repression, sublimation, rationalization, displacement, identification, and projection. Although many other concepts and theories of Freudian psychology are significant contributions to knowledge, their influence on American sociology is less pronounced than these views on motivation and personality development.

Weber

Of all the modern European intellectuals whose theories are studied by American sociologists, Weber apparently has exerted the dominant influence in recent years.[8] His conceptions of social action and methodology are his most fundamental contributions, though his accomplishments in economics, political science, social history, and comparative religion also impressed American sociologists.

Weber analyzes human conduct as *social action*. Thus all forms of group activity or organization are viewed as ultimately comprised of the actions of individuals whose subjective intentions orient their behavior toward the expectations of other persons. It is the task of sociology to explain social action through the special method of understanding (*Verstehen*), which permits interpretation of the subjective motivations of individual actors.

Assuming that such other-oriented individual conduct is dictated, in the ideal case, by rational appraisal of the situation for efficient realization of one's purpose, Weber set forth a classification of social action. Any concrete conduct may be identified with one or a combination of four ideal types of social action, two of which are of maximum rationality. *Purposive* or *expedient action* implies a choice of means calculated to achieve an end with greatest efficiency. However, such a goal is only one of several alternatives in social life and will be pursued only so long as excessive cost in sacrificing other ends is not required. *Value-prescribed action* delimits the choice of possible means in accordance with a single absolute end or value which is pursued irrespective of consequences. The two remaining types of action refer to behavior which is nonrational or irrational rather than primarily rational. Thus, *traditional action* requires the selection of means in keeping with the sanctity of the past (which tends to elevate means to the status of ends). In *emotional* or *affective action* means and ends are linked together in the expression of the actor's emotions or feeling-states. Whenever any type of social action involving two or more actors indicates a set of mutually oriented, subjectively intended expectations, a *social relationship* exists. Weber's fundamentally volitional, individualistic conception of social phenomena is extremely congenial to voluntaristic nominalism and thus makes his theory particularly attractive to American sociologists.

Weber's methodological arguments arrested the attention of several American sociologists during the development of systematic theory in the late 1930s. The subsequent dissemination and frequent acceptance of his methodological principles suggest their congeniality with much of American sociology. They are not only consistent with individualism generally, but are designed to make the social sciences as precise and certain as the natural sciences without relinquishing the distinctions between them. Accepting the traditional German contrast between the *Geisteswissenschaften* (social sciences) and the *Naturwissenschaften* (natural sciences), Weber argues that the precision attained in the natural sciences by strict mathematical methods can also be achieved in the social sciences by the use of logical analysis and procedure.

Furthermore, Weber denies that the natural sciences alone have a monopoly on generalized theoretical categories. This conviction, coupled with his emphasis on logic, led him to develop the methodological principle of *ideal types* for use in the social realm. Since social phenomena can be viewed from many perspectives, depending particularly upon the values involved in the situation and the original problem formulated by the investigator, they must be precisely conceptualized by the sociologist in order that systematic comparison with other social phenomena can be undertaken. An ideal type is thus a specifically defined, meaningful constellation which is genetic in nature (because it must contain the motives of action) and is a deliberate intensification and overemphasis of certain aspects of concrete events (because it is viewed from one selected perspective).

In his own writings Weber employs two major kinds of ideal types. On the one hand, he develops concepts of unique historical individuals or events, for example, modern capitalism which is characterized by the religious ethic of Protestantism. On the other hand, he isolates recurrent factors or common conditions such as rational-legal, traditional, and charismatic types of authority, which are present in various social situations or historical events.

Weber himself demonstrates the applicability of his methodological principles by extensive historical investigations. He studied the bureaucratic mode of social organization in modern Western society, analyzed social stratification, and compared the great world religions of Hinduism, Confucianism, and Christianity. Recently these empirical researches have also exercised considerable influence on American sociologists.

It may be surprising that the writings of Karl Marx, which stimulated Weber and many other European intellectuals, exercised relatively little influence on American sociology. Marx's explanations of class structure and its relation to social change, political institutions, the family, ideologies, science, and religion stimulated some sociologists in this country to examine these same topics, but usually led them to different conclusions. The basic reason for the nonacceptance of Marxist theories appears to derive from his economic determinism, which is often interpreted as a fundamental denial of American individualism and which is inconsistent with the multicausational position of most American sociologists.

In sum, the national emergencies of the third era in American sociology not only encouraged the application of scientific knowledge in the resolution of practical problems, but also contributed to the emergence of a new function for sociological theory. The resulting development of theory owes many of its ideas and basic principles to the sociological works of European scholars, especially Pareto, Durkheim, Freud, and Weber. Although some of the conceptions of these four men are incompatible with the problems, assumptions, and interests of modern American sociologists, others are very congenial, particularly those pertaining to the motivation of action, the interrelatedness of social wholes, the process of change, and scientific methodology. The significance of these timely contributions of European theorists is evident in the recent attempts at systematic theory construction based on the traditions of positivism or social action which are examined in the following pages.

Sociological Neo-Positivism: Lundberg

The leading exponent of neo-positivism in contemporary American sociology is George A. Lundberg. After receiving his M.A. and Ph.D. degrees at the Universities of Wisconsin and Minnesota, respectively, he embarked on a teaching and research career which carried him across the United States. He was a member of the faculties of the University of Pittsburgh, Columbia University, and Bennington College in the East. In 1945 he returned to the University of Washington (where he held his first academic appointment) to become Walker Ames Professor and head of the Department of Sociology.

Although Lundberg insists that sociologists must scrupulously separate their roles as scientists and citizens, he justifies sociology as a science on the grounds of its practical utility for obtaining social objectives. (But he avoids the question of *whose* objectives sociology should serve.) Like Comte, his positivistic predecessor, he views social disorganization as a consequence of the coexistence within society of inconsistent principles of knowledge—the theological, metaphysical, and scientific. Our social order might be re-organized and stabilized, he contends, on the basis of any one of these principles. However, the prevalent technologically-induced interdependence of our civilization, based largely on science, demands that scientific or positivistic principles be used. Sociology's ultimate instrumental function is to aid in this scientific reorganization of society.

As the science of human relations, sociology "can save us," though it cannot prescribe the ends men should seek or how the knowledge of the various sciences (including sociology) should be used.[9] But Lundberg is convinced that our common humanity confers general agreement on these ends and that conflict arises "over the means toward these ends, as represented by fantastic ideologies." Sociology's practical contribution is first, to formulate possible alternatives of action under given conditions and second, to indicate the means, expense, and near and remote consequences of alternative social policies. By demonstrating its ability to predict these consequences and to calculate the achievability, the costs, and the compatibility of men's aspirations, sociology can itself condition men's choices. The determination of probable effects of different social programs and policies requires knowledge of the "natural" laws of human behavior which are not limited to the conditions of specific cultures but possess the same universality as the laws of gravity. If men wish to achieve organization and peace, they must abide by the restrictions that these fundamental laws of conduct impose.

For sociology to provide reliable predictions it must reappraise its assumptions, concepts, techniques, and methodology in the light of the demands of natural science.[10] Lundberg concludes that mathematics, social measuring instruments, "operational definitions," a consistent frame of reference, and a logically coherent, empirically verifiable system of concepts are indispensable for the discovery of predictive sociological generalizations and laws.

These generalizations must involve enumeration, Lundberg argues, for they are statements of the probable prevalence of a social phenomenon or a configuration of social data. To attain maximum predictive value, generalizations must be stated mathematically. When these statements indicating the statistical probability of the occurrence of an event under specified conditions have been empirically verified, they become laws. Reliable, verifiable observations on which such generalizations are based require such standardized measuring instruments as attitude scales, opinion thermometers, and the like. Through instruments of this kind concepts may be defined in terms of the operations by which data are obtained, that is, "operationally." "Intelligence," for example, is *that which* intelligence tests measure or, in a different area, "opinion" is *that which* polling techniques provide. Lundberg claims that if concepts are to be standardized, communicable, and useful for science, this operational procedure is essential.

The content of concepts reflects the basic assumptions, axioms, and postulates of any discipline. As the frame of reference for sociology, these presuppositions should be rigorously examined to see if they meet the demands of natural science. Using arguments drawn from Pareto, Lundberg insists that this frame of reference must be organized so as to constitute the basis for a logically consistent and coherent abstract conceptual system.[11] The system of basic concepts should be applicable to all concrete situations, events, or behavior which sociology investigates. Through their combinations and permutations, these concepts furnish the basis for hypotheses and permit their systematic testing. Study along these lines provides the only adequate source of predictive generalizations in sociology.

The content of the frame of reference which Lundberg tries to establish for sociology is calculated to make the discipline a genuine *social physics* (to use Comte's term). Lundberg defines sociology as the study of interhuman activity, including intrahuman or "inner" behavior which has other people as a point of reference. This definition resembles the basic postulate of the social action frame of reference, to be considered shortly. However, Lundberg regards interhuman activity as a system of energy within a field of force, changes in which are fundamentally forms of energy transformation within the physical cosmos—like changes in other aspects of the universe. Observable social behavior is viewed as the consequence of energy-determining attractions or repulsions and similarities or dissimilarities (such as status, age, sex, beliefs, and economic position) operating within a field of force. Included in this field are the behavior in question and the total environment—a situation to be investigated as a "closed system."

Lundberg's social-physical (or natural science) conception of human society represents an adaptation of the theories of Frederic Le Play and Patrick Geddes, although it had been worked out independently by Stuart Dodd, now Lundberg's colleague. Without attempting to introduce Dodd's detailed mathematical symbolism, Lundberg agrees with the latter that any social situation can be described in terms of the formula: "(S)ocial situation equals (P)opulations with certain (I)ndicators of characteristics changing in (T)ime and/or spatial (L)ength"; or $S = P:I:T:L$. Population may be classified as social categories and types of groups. Indicators involve the basic social process of communication (expressed in association and dissociation), institutions, and demographic variations. The time variable, or societal change, involves processes and factors of change such as invention. The spatial variable, or (L)ength, includes factors and processes of human ecology. In their various possible combinations these four fundamental, generalized conceptual variables (P,I,T,L) should serve to describe any social situation or form of interhuman activity. More specialized concepts, their operational definitions, construction of measuring devices, and the derivation of hypotheses for empirical verification in research should use as their starting point these four basic concepts of the natural science system of human society.

Lundberg's continuing endeavor to develop a sociology modeled upon the physical sciences, especially physics, has had considerable influence among younger sociologists. His emphasis on the use of statistical procedures is in keeping with efforts to conduct sociological research more rigorously and with greater precision. But the implications of behaviorism and so-called physicalism in his position still seem to contradict the pervasive voluntarism of American sociology. Appropriately, a vigorous opposition has come from the exponents of the social action theory which is now to be surveyed. (Moreover, it is legitimate to regard the disagreement between the neo-positivist Lundberg and the social action theorists as a continuation of the subjectivism-objectivism controversy of the late 1920s and the early 1930s. MacIver, who is currently associated with the social action viewpoint, defended the position of subjectivism—indicated in Chapter Two—while Lundberg was a protagonist of objectivism and statistics.) [12]

Social Action Theory

Since World War II social action theory (as noted earlier, not to be confused with social reform efforts) has become the dominant theoretical perspective in American sociology. In addition to the obvious advantage of having its principal proponents strategically located in leading university centers, this orientation owes its ascendance, at least in part, to its adoption and further development of a unified, logically consistent and integrated system and, it may be argued, to its commitment to an essentially voluntaristic, individualistic interpretation of social behavior traditional in American sociology (which neo-positivism, by its association with behaviorism, seems to threaten or question).

Four sociologists—Florian Znaniecki, Robert M. MacIver, Howard P. Becker, and Talcott Parsons—have been primarily responsible for the development of social action theory in this country, though its intellectual antecedents go back ultimately to German idealist social science traditions and, more immediately, to Max Weber in particular. Of the four, Becker and Parsons have most explicitly credited Weber as inspiring their theoretical formulations. But whether directly influenced or not, all four scholars are in fundamental agreement with Weber's conception of social action as conduct guided by awareness of other persons whose behavior is regarded by the actor as affecting attainment of his own ends. From this postulate various implications have been deduced, which together constitute what has come to be termed the *action frame of reference*.

The first proposition of this frame of reference or set of assumptions, in which Znaniecki, MacIver, Becker, and Parsons concur, holds that group behavior must be referred back to, and becomes meaningful in terms of, the subjective intentions of the individual participants. Conduct toward others is impelled by motives.* It aims at the attainment of purposes, ends, or goals. Social action involves the satisfaction of wishes, attitudes, or dispositions in the form of values and interests. It seeks, argues Parsons, to optimize gratification and minimize deprivations. Other-directed activity is thus individually *teleological* in nature.

---

* All of the theorists under consideration are interested in the study of motives in relation to social control and cultural prescriptions. MacIver specifically regards the investigation of individual motives (as distinct from social pressures or sanctions) as a psychological task not within the province of sociology.

A second proposition of the action frame of reference states that goal-oriented conduct occurs in a situation, at a specific place and time. Aspects of the situation which are unchangeable are *conditions* with which any actor must reckon, whereas the aspects which can be changed and manipulated by the actor in attaining his goals are the *means*.

A third proposition in this set of assumptions, to which only Becker seems to express clear dissent, maintains that there are always alternative means to ends or alternative ends themselves which require exercise of choice. This view finds its expression in the recurrent use of the terms *selection, evaluation, judgment,* and (dynamic) *assessment*. However, choice in human conduct is neither wholly random nor entirely circumscribed by conditions: it tends to be limited by social codes, cultural standards, and institutional norms.

Although other propositions about social conduct may be deduced from the definition given above, the minimal components of the action frame of reference are means, ends, conditions, and norms. Parsons, in fact, views them as comprising the terms of the unit act—the fundamental datum of sociological study.

The social action approach also implies that sociologists should study material that symbolizes or expresses the subjective intentions of actors. Thus Znaniecki, MacIver, Becker, and Parsons agree that information drawn from the actor's own testimony is of basic importance in analyzing the determinants of conduct. According to Znaniecki and MacIver, the sociologist is justified in using data from the person's own experience because the individual is aware of himself and others as conscious personalities (that is, he is characterized by what Znaniecki calls the "humanistic coefficient"). MacIver's view that the individual's own testimony should be invoked to aid in the "sympathetic reconstruction" of the factors involved in behavior is consistent with his insistence that consciousness or awareness is an intrinsic aspect of social relationships (as distinct from nonsocial relationships of the type studied in the physical sciences).

In short, Znaniecki, MacIver, Becker, and Parsons concur in their basic views on social action. They accept Weber's conception of social action. They agree that means, ends, conditions, and institutional norms are basic components of the social action system. And all of them urge the use of data drawn from the actor's own perspective and experience as indispensable to fruitful analysis of social behavior. Since social action as a logical system has been elaborated in different directions, the particular contributions of each theorist must now be examined.

Znaniecki

Although Florian Znaniecki's uninterrupted participation in American sociological circles began only in 1939, his work had been known for some time through his publications, especially *The Polish Peasant in Europe and America* (1918–1920), of which he was co-author with W. I. Thomas, and his teaching as a visiting professor at the University of Chicago and Columbia University. Until World War II he had been a member of the faculty of the University of Poznan in Poland, the country in which he was born and received his training in philosophy and sociology. In 1940 he joined the Sociology Department of the University of Illinois, where he taught until his recent retirement. His major fields of sociological study are methodology, sociology of knowledge, nationalism, the nature and history of social thought, and sociological theory.[13]

Znaniecki's *Social Actions* (1936) and *Cultural Sciences* (1952) are especially devoted to the analysis of the structure and processes of social action. In any social situation, Znaniecki observes, the individual or agent tries to affect the behavior of a *social object*, the primary human target who is crucial to the agent's purposes. The agent attempts to influence the social object by using certain *social instruments* (or mechanisms at his disposal in the situation) in a certain fashion called the *social method*. The modification of the activities of the object as they appear to the agent is termed the *social reaction*. To a salesman, for example, the potential customer is a social object. The desired reaction, sale of an article, may be secured by the method of persuasively flattering the customer. Advertising, price lists, even the product itself may be used as instruments to effect a sale.

Any particular action is based on the subject's or agent's conception of the possibilities to be actualized or prevented in the situation in accordance with his purposes. This *definition of the situation* depends on his own attitudes and on relevant *standards of value* and *norms of conduct*. The agent thus normally believes that there are certain standards by which people and things in the situation should be valued and certain norms according to which people ought to act in the situation. When he and others in the situation behave in conformity with these standards and norms, their actions are patterned. Znaniecki calls such ordered actions *axionormative*, for both standards of value and norms have been applied to the conduct.

Nonconformist behavior results when persons' actions deviate further from the ideals than the permissible variation. These transgressions of recognized standards and values are causes of *cultural disorganization* which, in turn, requires *cultural reorganization*. Members of action systems ordinarily try to counteract violations by various forms of repression, such as banishment and imprisonment. Often the participation of representatives or members of an action system in punishing transgressors serves to strengthen the solidarity and accentuate the conformity of the group. This effect is termed a *conservative reorganization* of the action system. For example, the fact that the Spanish branch of the Roman Catholic Church is more conservative and stricter in its conformity than other branches of the Church may be the consequence of its conflict with Islam, the expulsion of the Jews and Moors, and its active opposition to Protestantism. An action system may undergo *creative reorganization*, a second type, by the gradual introduction of new values, cultural patterns of action, or new relationships of functional interdependence. Cooperation comes to replace former conflict within or between action systems.

These ordered (organized) and disordered (disorganized) actions involve various processes which are dependent on the actor's appraisal of the social object's attitudes toward the actor's own purposes. Those actions arising from a favorable evaluation of the social object's attitudes toward the subject's ends are classified as forms of accommodation, for they require some mutual adjustment of activities and attitudes. (This process is further subdivided on the basis of whether or not the person shows initiative or passivity in evoking the object's positive reactions.) If the person in question believes that the object is negatively disposed toward the attainment of his ends, his action is a form of opposition, either defensive or aggressive. When the individual acts positively because he is favorably inclined toward the object for the object's own sake, the action is a type of altruism. To act only for the sake of harming the object is a form of hostility.

Znaniecki's basic methodology and conception of social causation most closely resemble the views of Robert M. MacIver, a personal friend and colleague during Znaniecki's lectureship at Columbia University. In view of their intellectual similarity, it is now appropriate to consider MacIver's contribution to social action theory.

MacIver

Like Znaniecki, MacIver is not a native American sociologist. He was born in Scotland where he also acquired his intellectual training and early academic experience. After receiving his doctorate at the University of Edinburgh, he taught at the University of Aberdeen. Later he went to Canada to join the University of Toronto faculty and from there he came to Columbia University in 1927. During his more than twenty years of academic life at Columbia he was especially active in studying political sociology, intergroup relations, and social action theory.[14] His principal contributions to action theory include a methodological theory, classification of social structures, a typology of societies, and interpretations of social change and social causation.

MacIver's social action theory is ultimately based on his conception of social relationships. As the field of study for sociology, social relationships differ from physical and organic relationships in being determined by the mutual recognition of beings endowed with consciousness. Since mutual recognition requires that individuals be subjectively aware of other persons as objects, MacIver's conception of social relationships necessarily involves the subject-object distinction of social action theory. To use MacIver's own terms, both "attitudes," or subjective dispositions toward objects, and "interests," or objects toward which attitudes are directed, are involved in social behavior. Attitudes are primarily associative and dissociative. Interests are like and common. *Like interests* are enjoyed or pursued distributively or separately by each individual privately, whereas *common interests* must be sought collectively and shared without division. The like interest may be illustrated by the credits toward which college students work. But the college life in which they participate is shared. Of course, the like may also become the basis for common interest. In addition, common interests are divided into two types which are particularly relevant to the analysis of social relationships. The first entails identification of men with some inclusive, indivisible social unity, such as in-group loyalty to an ethnic group. The second type involves attachment to some impersonal goal or endeavor, for example, the furtherance of the prohibitionist cause. MacIver's general concept of common interest further emphasizes the fundamental subject-object difference between attitudes and interests. Attitudes may be harmonious, but they cannot be common, for the subjective element is always individualized and private. But people can have common interests, just as they have common possessions.

Since the individual experiences groups as objects to be used in attaining ends or as constraints on his conduct, MacIver's concept of interest is the point of departure for classifying social groups into three principal varieties. The first general type involves inclusive social groupings which occupy a limited territory and are characterized by unspecialized interests. Community, the generic type, is an unplanned inclusive network of relationships arising from the sharing of the basic conditions of common living on a common soil. The second general type includes social groupings conscious of general interests which have not, however, crystallized into permanent and definite organizations. Class, ethnic, and racial groups, and crowds are generic types. Social groupings with specific interests and specific and enduring organizations constitute the third general type. These groups are organized purposefully to attain a distinct interest. The generic type is the association, with the primary group and large-scale association as the two subtypes. Using interest as a criterion, these two subvarieties are further divided into primary and secondary forms. Primary interests, which are the basis for primary groups, are cultural in nature and are pursued for their own sake, for direct satisfaction. Secondary interests, which are the basis for large-scale associations, are utilitarian and civilizational in nature, and are desired because they are *means* to satisfactions. Large-scale associations are further classified as economic, political, and technological.

Implicit in the typology just outlined is an evolutionary formulation of social change. In its earlier phases society as a social structure was *communal*. More recently, society has become *associational*, with groups of the third general type conspicuous in its organization. This change is evolutionary in that increasing differentiation (and integration) are entailed.*

Communal or primitive society is characterized by "primitive fusion." Utilitarian means and cultural ends are integrated. The instruments of making a living are pervasively intertwined with customs and tradition. The society is an inclusive community unified by blood or kinship and by occupation of a common territory. Membership in the few social groupings, based on kinship, age, or sex criteria, is obligatory. Age and sex differences are the primary bases for division of labor. Large-scale voluntary associations do not exist.

Later, certain social functions tend to become vested in particular subgroups in the society. The rights and privileges attached to such functions as religious or magical activities come to be distinguished from the general, customary codes. Thus specific modes of procedures, or new *institutions*, are formed. MacIver terms this intermediate phase the *stage of differentiated communal institutions*.

Associational, or modern, civilized society is socially differentiated. Means and ends are separated into two distinctive realms, and primitive fusion has been destroyed. Culture itself is no longer bound to the land or to the kinship groups. The now elaborate division of labor is in intricate func-

---

* Division of labor has increased so that specialization and functional interdependence have become more intricate. Each of the functional associations and institutions, which become more numerous and varied, is specific and limited in its range of services. And, finally, the instruments of communication have become more diverse and refined.

tional interdependence. The emergence of large-scale associations, voluntarily organized in accordance with specialized interests, implies the accomplishment of the intellectually difficult feat of combining likenesses and differences. Since society no longer integrates values for the individual, choice must be exercised. Society itself is characterized by a unity which is multiform rather than uniform.

For MacIver the process of social change as well as social causation itself depends on the operation of *dynamic assessment*. Social change is initiated by the changing choices or judgments of interrelated individuals who interpret, evaluate, or assess situations. Any one or more of four factors which impinge on the choices in and appraisals of the situation may lead to social change. Alteration in the cultural system of values governing the selection of goals or aims; in the society's utilitarian devices and techniques providing means for ends; in the social relations acting as an agency, obstacle, or goal of action; and in the physical-organic conditions relevant to and necessary for attaining a goal—all are sources of change. But these factors are dynamic only as they are subjectively apprehended and assessed and brought into a coherent and consistent unity by individuals and groups.

MacIver is one of the two exponents of social action who are fundamentally preoccupied with the problem of social change. Howard Becker, the other, has made the explanation of social change the central concern of his analytic scheme.

Becker

Howard Becker is the only social action theorist who is American both by birth and by academic training. He was a student of the late Professor Robert E. Park at the University of Chicago, where he received his Ph.D. Since 1937 he has been a professor of sociology at the University of Wisconsin. Throughout his career he has been especially preoccupied with the history of social thought and the development of sociological theory.[15] His persistent interest in the problem of social change is illustrated by his published study of the German youth movement and in unpublished researches on German peasant villages and the mentality of the ancient Greeks, among other writings.

Apart from the constructed type methodology, Becker's principal theoretical contribution consists of his application of social action theory to the study of social change. His action theory makes use of G. H. Mead's interpretation of the significance of symbols, Max Weber's types of relations between means and ends, Znaniecki's differentiation of the components of an action situation, and W. I. Thomas' four wishes.

According to Becker, the specific values of the larger society are the context for social action in any concrete situation. These values are a context because they have become interwoven in the personality in the course of past socialization. Needs of any normally socialized person are both culturally and interpersonally defined by the shared cultural values. Learning the culture requires the acquisition of symbols which, in turn, is possible only by direct personal interaction and role-playing. Accordingly, the socialized individual's needs are necessarily defined and satisfied through ends or purposes oriented to others and through values shared with others by communication. By a transformation of Thomas' scheme of the four wishes, Becker classifies the final ends of action as new experience, response, recognition, and security. Both needs and ends of social action are related to values by use of Mead's interpretation of the role of the symbol. Since social action is value-defined action, its analysis—contends Becker—entails study of the impact of the society's value system on the concrete circumstances of action.

To interpret the specific course of goal-oriented action in a given situation, Becker employs analytic distinctions earlier devised by Znaniecki and Weber. In accordance with Znaniecki's analysis of the action situation, Becker notes that any actor will be oriented toward a social object or person and will select a particular method and an instrument or instruments to try to evoke a desired social response from the social object. Becker also uses Weber's means-ends typology to classify the possible relationships between means (Znaniecki's method and instruments) and ends (the purposes of the actor). If a person's choice of means to attain a certain end is governed only by considerations of minimizing effort and undesirable consequences and maximizing efficiency, the means-ends relationship is termed *expedient rationality*. "Cold-blooded calculation" is its hallmark. When the end itself limits or prescribes the kinds of means which can be used (over and beyond mere efficiency), the means-ends relationship is called *sanctioned rationality*. For example, the Christian ethic forbids the use of force in making one love one's neighbor as one's self. In the third type, *traditional nonrationality*, what were once means are elevated to the rank of ends. The role of the fasces in recent times as contrasted with its role in Roman military discipline is illustrative. The *fasces*, an axe with a number of rods lashed about it, is now a commonly employed emblem of unchanging justice, whereas it was once used to discipline Roman soldiers. *Affective nonrationality*, the fourth type, represents a fairly complete fusion of means and ends when it is incorporated as a chief phase of an action. It includes everything from outbursts of love or hatred to the unquestioning, emotionalized acceptance of a leader.

All of these conceptual distinctions—personal needs, cultural values, means, ends, means-ends relationships—are utilized in Becker's analysis of social change. For this purpose Becker also amplifies and elaborates the conceptions of sacred and secular societies earlier proposed by Park. As constructed types, the sacred-secular dichotomy can be applied to the investigation of concrete societies. In a sacred society the value systems, social action, and personalities are characterized by a maximum aversion to change, by a tendency to respond negatively, or to reject the new as it is defined in the society. Because the society is spatially, socially, and mentally isolated, its value system is rigid and relatively impermeable. Its members seek the ends of response, recognition, and especially security. The means by which these ends are sought are primarily those of traditional nonrationality and sanctioned rationality. In contrast, the value systems, social action, and personalities of a secular society show a maximum of readiness and capacity to change, to respond positively, or to accept the new as it is defined in the society. Since the society is spatially, socially, and mentally accessible to the stimuli of change, its value systems are flexible and permeable. Recognition, response, and especially new experience are the desired ends of its members, which are attained primarily by the means of expedient rationality and affective nonrationality.

Each of these two types of society is further divided into subtypes. If a sacred society shows a diffuse opposition to change because it is tradition-bound and invokes traditionally nonrational means, it is classified as a folk- (or traditional) sacred society. Many preliterate societies, though not all, fall into this subtype. The Alabama and Missouri communities described by H. C. Nixon in *Possum Trot: Rural Community, South* (1941) and by James West in *Plainville, U.S.A.* (1945) also belong in this category. If the antagonism to change becomes organized and specified by a set of rigid, explicit prescriptions and injunctions and if the society tends to use means of the sanctioned rationality variety, it is a prescribed- (or sanctioned) sacred society. A totalitarian kind of structure usually results, such as the Geneva theocracy of Calvin, the Jesuit state of Paraguay, Nazi Germany, Fascist Italy, and Soviet Russia. A secular society which is inclined to favor change consistent with certain flexible, generalized principles and which often tends to use expediently rational means to attain security as the dominant end is a principled- (or stable) secular society. The social life of middle-class urban Americans is suggestive of this variety. When change is welcomed simply because it is new, when new experience is the dominant end sought by affectively nonrational means, the society is termed a norm-less- (or unstable) secular society. Modern "emancipated" circles of cosmopolitan urban centers are the closest approximation to this type. Admittedly, there is a point beyond which even an extreme secular society cannot go if it is to remain a society. Something sacred must persist—some goals in common, a value system with ends in some respects shared—for a collection of human beings pursuing at random a systemless mass of discrete ends is scarcely a society.

These four major types of societies represent points on a continuum of sacredness and secularity. Any concrete society can thus be examined with reference to its position on this continuum. The impact of particular social changes can be interpreted as producing more or less sacralization or secularization in the society.

Becker's action theory, as well as those of Znaniecki and MacIver, stands in contrast to the social system formulation of Talcott Parsons, the last of the major action theorists whose intellectual position is now to be outlined. Of the four sociologists, only Parsons explicitly incorporates in his theory implications drawn from Freud and Pareto.

Parsons

Talcott Parsons, who was born in the United States and received his doctorate in economics from the University of Heidelberg (Germany), is an unusually influential social action theorist. He has contributed well-known analyses of kinship, social stratification, political movements, mass communications, and the professions, especially medicine.[16] But his recent development of a theory of the social system has evoked particularly widespread comment in American sociology.[17] In 1946 Parsons became the first chairman of the new interdisciplinary Department of Social Relations at Harvard University where he had been teaching since 1927.

Like Lundberg, Parsons accepts Pareto's view that an abstract system of concepts is required for the scientific study and analysis of social phenomena. But he differs from Lundberg in using the action frame of reference, or set of assumptions about social behavior, for deriving the concepts which are the categories or parts of his logically closed system. Combining aspects of the theories of Kant, Weber, and Freud, Parsons proposes that any study of social relations must start with an actor (or subject) who is oriented to a situation composed of physical, cultural, and social objects. The subject's action is prompted by one or a combination of three modes of motivational orientation. The *cognitive mode* involves cognition or an interest in knowing or defining aspects of the situation. The *cathectic mode* indicates cathexis or an interest in securing maximum gratification of needs-dispositions. And the *evaluative mode* refers to evaluation or to interest in ordered choice from the possible objects in the situation.

With this conception of the action frame of reference, Parsons undertakes the analysis of social behavior. He observes that the interaction of two persons is entirely different from the action of a single action oriented to a nonsocial object. Social objects (other persons) can respond and, therefore, can affect the gratification which the particular person is seeking. Hence the action of any individual toward another person must always take into consideration what alternatives are open to the other individual and that his own choices will influence what the other person decides to do. The obverse is true for the other person—the social object. Accordingly, each individual is oriented to the expectations of the other persons in social interaction. Stable interactions require a shared common set of moral standards so that each individual knows what to expect from the other in the situation. When these stable and regulated motivated interactions of two or more actors are oriented toward one another and toward a collective goal so that they constitute an organized system, they are termed a *social system*.

The basic unit of the social system as well as the smallest stable sector of situationally specific interactions is the *role*. Actual overt conduct of an individual as a member of a group in a socially defined situation comprises a role. However, the actor's conduct is guided by a shared moral standard of what he and other individuals believe he ought to do. Ordinarily he is motivated to conform to this role-expectation, for the rule will have been incorporated in his personality during his earlier socialization. He now regards adherence to the expected conduct as the normal way to fulfil his needs. He feels pride in living up to the dictates of his conscience. And, moreover, he wants and needs the social approval which can be secured by conformity. For example, part of the role of a member of a delinquent gang is to refuse to "squeal" on the others if he is caught by the police. He has learned that the way to be a success is to abide by the code. He expects to gain social commendation from other members for conforming to the rule and, conversely, he feels shame if he unwittingly divulges information to the legal authorities. The actual role will tend to coincide with the role-expectation if the rule or standard involved has been institutionalized. This process of *institutionalization* has occurred if conformity to the role-expectation has become a way of satisfying the needs of any actor as well as a condition for maximizing the gratifications of other persons in the situation. Thus, Parsons' concept of role interlocks motivation, gratification, and choice with the prevalence of shared standards and stability.

Furthermore, the social system is comprised of various kinds of roles or constellations of roles which are termed *institutions*. Only through the performance of differentiated roles can the social system operate as a system. The nature of minimum roles is prescribed by the conditions which any self-subsistent social system must meet if it is to persist. These necessary conditions, or *functional prerequisites*, are set by the scarcity of desired objects in any action situation, the nature of the human organism, and the realities of orderly coexistence among the actors in a situation.

Parsons outlines four general types of institutions or constellations of roles which are common to self-subsistent social systems or societies. Based on the subject-object distinction in the frame of reference, *relational* institutions classify and limit the roles which actors may legitimately assume as subjects and as objects (apart from their interest in one another). Parsons subdivides these institutions into orientation roles, or subject roles, and object roles, or roles played as objects of orientation. *Regulative* institutions classify and limit the roles which actors may legitimately assume with reference to goals and means of one another's interests. Claims to objects, either as *facilities* (objects desired for the uses to which they can be put) or as *rewards* (objects desired for their own sake, as direct ends of gratification), must be institutionally regulated if the social system is to persist in equilibrium. Economic and political institutions regulate access to facilities and social stratification regulates access to rewards. *Integrative* institutions fulfil the functional prerequisite of negative and positive coordination in the social system. These institutions prevent disruptive interferences among the roles and facilitate the achievement of shared goals through collective action. So-called responsibility roles for both private and public interests are included in this type of institution. *Cultural* institutions are distinctive in that they involve acceptance of value patterns rather than commitments to action. Science, religion, philosophy, and art are classified as cultural institutions.*

Just as motivation to conform is crucial to the ordered performance of roles embodied in these four types of institutions, so deviant motivation is the source of change in the social system. Social change is ultimately a problem of individual deviations which have become so recurrent and focalized that mechanisms of social control are no longer effective. The lack of coincidence of individual gratifications with shared role-expectations is the basic mechanism for explaining the impetus to change, its persistence and extension, and stabilization in the social system.

Parsons' theoretical formulations have had widespread intellectual repercussions in American sociology. His influence has been exercised both through his own publications and those of his students, such as Marion Levy and Wilbert Moore of Princeton University, Robin Williams of Cornell University, and Kingsley Davis and Robert Merton of Columbia University. Though all of these sociologists have made independent contributions, Merton's theory and research have particularly provoked sociological comment and discussion.

---

* This usage of the word *culture* is consistent with that of R. M. MacIver.

Theories of the Middle Range: Merton

Robert K. Merton, professor of sociology at Columbia University since 1941, has an intellectual orientation both similar to and different from that of Talcott Parsons, his former teacher. Like Parsons, he regards science as an abstract, generalized theoretical system of logically consistent and inter-dependent assumptions, concepts, and propositions; his theory is also based on the means-ends scheme of social action; and his analytic paradigm, or statement of prescriptions for conducting research, is used in the same way as Parsons employs his elaborate theoretical system.

Merton differs conspicuously from Parsons in his view about the level at which profitable theorization can now occur. He does not agree that soci-ology should seek an integrated or master conceptual scheme at present. He declares, rather, that the discipline can advance only by devoting major concern to what are known as *theories of the middle range,* that is, those intermediate to routine research hypotheses and an inclusive conceptual system. This level involves special theories applicable to limited ranges of data, for example, theories about social class, bureaucracy, and interper-sonal influence.

Although he hardly depreciates theory, Merton seems to be somewhat more acutely sensitive to empirical fact and research in sociological inquiry than is Parsons. Indeed, he insists that theory and research are reciprocally interrelated in science. His formulation of their interrelations has been so favorably received that textbooks in methods of social research are now in-corporating it.[18]

Recognizing that any investigation is conducted on the basis of certain assumptions, Merton contends that the researcher's orientation should be made explicit as an analytic paradigm. He urges use of the paradigm to prevent unwitting importation of outside assumptions into the research, to facilitate the codification of methods, and to aid in accumulating theoreti-cal interpretations and in sensitizing the sociologist to related theoretical or empirical problems.

Merton follows Parsons in accepting a functionalist conception of society. His analytic paradigm is also functionalist. But Merton's paradigm does not show the theoretical comprehensiveness or logical elaborateness of Parsons' social system, for Merton is committed to middle-range theories. Accordingly, Merton's paradigm stipulates only the minimum requirements for the functional study of social structure and change. Nevertheless, he describes eleven separate aspects of functional analysis, involving specifica-tion of assumptions, concepts, analytic procedures, and methods of valida-tion.[19]

The most crucial of all of these aspects is the identification of function.[20] But an understanding of function is impossible without the knowledge, as the functional theorist conceives it, of society as an operating whole of in-terrelated and interdependent parts. The components of society act and react on one another and on the entire system. These actions tend to have objective consequences for the organization of a society. An objective con-sequence of a social or cultural item (such as a role or status) which con-tributes to the survival, persistence, integration, or stability of the society as a whole is a *function*. If such an effect, however, contributes to the disintegration or instability of the society or any of its segments and lessens its possibility of survival and persistence, it is termed a *dysfunction*. When the positive objective consequences are intended and recognized by persons involved, such effects are called *manifest functions*. If they are unintended and unrecognized, they are termed *latent functions*.

The inclusion of the concept of dysfunction in the paradigm is very important, for it indicates how the study of social change may be approached from a functionalist perspective. The instability characterizing dysfunction suggests stress, strain, tension, and disequilibrium—the social conditions out of which deviation and change may arise in a social system.

Although the concept of dysfunction is not the specific point of departure for Merton's paper "Social Structure and Anomie," it is concretely illustrated in this essay on change and reactions to change. Here Merton is especially concerned with the emergence of deviant forms of role adaptations in a social structure, such as contemporary American society, which places a disproportionate emphasis on the cultural goals as opposed to the institutional rules regulating realization of goals. These deviant forms include *innovation* (the use of institutionally forbidden but effective means of attaining accepted goals), *ritualism* (abandonment of lofty goals accompanied by meticulous adherence to institutional rules), *retreatism* (passive withdrawal from sanctioned cultural goals and institutional means), and *rebellion* (rejection of both prevailing goals and means and the active effort to institute different goals and means).

Merton employs various aspects of the generalized functional paradigm in other studies of modern American society. His inquiries concentrate on certain phases of modern mass organization: bureaucracy, mass communications, and the social consequences of science.[21] Using functional analysis, he interprets two problems of contemporary bureaucratic structure. He suggests how such organizations develop a formalistic, ritualistic adherence to procedure, which is dysfunctional to the point of vitiating the actual purpose of the structure, as well as how strains are evoked in the structure by recruitment of social scientists as bureaucrats.

Merton's concern with the functional interdependence of thought and belief and social structure leads him to define the relations between the two related, though distinct, fields of the sociology of knowledge and the sociology of mass communications. *Mass Persuasion*, which is a study of the Kate Smith marathon radio war-bond drive of September, 1943, exemplifies the use of functional inquiry in mass communications. The war-bond drive is analyzed as an interdependent conjuncture of: (1) the immediate situation (a radio marathon) as a device for riveting the attention of a large audience upon a single person; (2) the content of the appeals (or themes) communicated by that person (Kate Smith) and the audience response to the themes; (3) the congruency of the public images of the figure with the emotional meanings of war bonds; (4) the predispositions of the audience subjected to persuasive appeals; (5) and the social and cultural setting to which the symbolism of appeal and personality traits are attached.

Merton's studies of the reciprocal relation between science and society have required both historical and contemporary settings. In the development of science during the early modern era, Merton is able convincingly to demonstrate the role of such social variables as religious belief (English and American Puritanism and later German Pietism), economic incentives, and technological improvements. Conversely, he examines the strains which science has produced in contemporary society, the generalized loci of conflict between science and modern society, as well as the more specific antagonisms provoked by opposition to the ethics of science and by the social dislocations resulting from the technological applications of science.

To some sociologists, Merton has achieved an unusually successful balance between theory construction and empirical research. Yet Parsons, Becker, MacIver, Znaniecki, and Lundberg have also contended—with varying emphasis—that systematic theory and concrete investigations are mutually required in scientific sociology. Various aspects of conceptual framework are being tested and refined by American sociologists studying bureaucracy, mass communications, intergroup relations, kinship, military life, political movements, professions, religion, social stratification, and small groups. Since this trend is likely to continue, present-day students of sociology will find it advantageous to acquire proficiency in the use of analytical systems of sociological theorists.

Footnotes to Chapter Three

1. Odum, Howard W.: *American Sociology*, New York, Longmans, Green & Co., Inc., 1951, p. 435.
2. Pareto, Vilfredo: *Mind and Society*. Translated and edited by Arthur Livingston, 4 Vols., New York, Harcourt, Brace & Co., 1935. See also the following excellent discussions of Pareto's work, Henderson, Lawrence J.: *Pareto's General Sociology*, Cambridge, Mass., Harvard University Press, 1935; Parsons, Talcott: *The Structure of Social Action*, Glencoe, Ill., The Free Press, 1949, Chaps. V, VI, and VII.
3. Durkheim, Émile: *The Division of Labor in Society*. Translated by George Simpson, Glencoe, Ill., The Free Press, 1949; *The Rules of Sociological Method*. Translated by Sarah A. Solovay and John H. Mueller and edited by George E. G. Catlin. Glencoe, Ill., The Free Press, 1950; *The Elementary Forms of the Religious Life*. Translated by Joseph W. Swain. Glencoe, Ill., The Free Press, 1947; Alpert, Harry: *Émile Durkheim and His Sociology*, New York, Columbia University Press, 1939; Parsons, Talcott: *The Structure of Social Action*, Glencoe, Ill., The Free Press, 1949, Chaps. VIII, IX, X and XI.
4. This concept is found in Durkheim, Emile: *Suicide*. Translated and edited by John A. Spaulding and George Simpson. Glencoe, Ill., The Free Press, 1951. This book is of interest to sociologists not only for its discussion of the problem of suicide but especially for its research procedures.
5. For a detailed analysis of the history of psychoanalysis in American sociology see: Hinkle, Gisela J.: "The Role of Freudianism in American Sociology." Unpublished Ph.D. dissertation, University of Wisconsin, 1951.
6. For a representative selection of Freud's works see Freud, Sigmund: *An Outline of Psychoanalysis*, New York, W. W. Norton & Co., Inc., 1949; Brill, A. A.: *The Basic Writings of Sigmund Freud*, New York, Modern Library, Inc., 1938. In his *Man in Society* (Studies in Sociology), New York, Random House, Inc., 1954, pp. 39–44, George Simpson has an excellent summary of psychoanalysis and its relevance to sociology.

7. Parsons, Talcott, Robert F. Bales, and Edward A. Shils: *Working Papers in the Theory of Action*, Glencoe, Ill., The Free Press, 1953.

8. Most of Max Weber's major works have now been translated. ———— *General Economic History*. Translated by Frank H. Knight. London, Allen and Unwin, Ltd., 1927; *The Protestant Ethic and the Spirit of Capitalism*. Translated by Talcott Parsons. London, Allen and Unwin, Ltd., 1930; *The Theory of Social and Economic Organization*. Translated and edited by Talcott Parsons and A. M. Henderson. New York, Oxford University Press, 1947; *Essays in Sociology*. Translated and edited by H. H. Gerth and C. W. Mills. New York, Oxford University Press, 1946; *The Methodology of the Social Sciences*. Translated by E. A. Shils and H. A. Finch, Glencoe, Ill., The Free Press, 1949; *The Religion of China: Confucianism and Taoism*. Translated by H. H. Gerth. Glencoe, Ill., The Free Press, 1951; *Ancient Judaism*. Translated by H. H. Gerth and Don Martindale. Glencoe, Ill., The Free Press, 1952.

For summaries of Weber's work see Parsons: Talcott: *The Structure of Social Action*, Glencoe, Ill., 1949, Chaps. XIV, XV, XVI, and XVII.

9. For a popular account of this position, see Lundberg, George: *Can Science Save Us?*, New York, Longmans, Green & Co., Inc., 1947.

10. This analysis of Lundberg is based on his *Foundations of Sociology*, New York, The Macmillan Co., 1939. The more recent *Sociology*, which was written with Clarence C. Schrag and Otto N. Larsen and published in New York by Harper & Brothers, 1954, does not seem to indicate any major alterations in Lundberg's own position as here presented. In addition to the two volumes mentioned and *Can Science Save Us?*, Lundberg is the author of *Social Research, A Study in Methods of Gathering Data*, New York, Longmans, Green and Co., Inc., 1942; co-author with Mirra Komarovsky and Mary Alice McInery of *Leisure: A Suburban Study*, New York, Columbia University Press, 1934; and co-editor with Read Bain and Nels Anderson of *Trends in American Sociology*, New York, Harper & Brothers, 1929; and is as well author of numerous articles in sociological and other scientific journals.

11. Lundberg, George A.: *Foundations of Sociology*, New York, The Macmillan Co., 1939, pp. 90, 113, and footnotes ♯4 on pp. 126–127 and ♯29 on p. 132.

12. For an account of the contemporary methodological dispute between neo-positivism and social action theory, see Simpson, George: *Man in Society* (Studies in Sociology), New York, Random House, Inc., 1954, pp. 48–60.

13. The following are Znaniecki's principal publications in English: *Cultural Reality*, Chicago, Ill., University of Chicago Press, 1919; *The Laws of Social Psychology*, Chicago, Ill., University of Chicago Press, 1925; *The Method of Sociology*, New York, Farrar & Rinehart, Inc., 1934; *Social Actions*, New York, Farrar & Rinehart, Inc., 1936; *The Social Role of the Man of Knowledge*, New York, Columbia University Press, 1940; *Modern Nationalities, a Sociological Study*, Urbana, Ill., University of Illinois, 1952; *Cultural Sciences, Their Origin and Development*, Urbana, Ill., University of Illinois, 1952; and Thomas, William I., and Florian Znaniecki: *The Polish Peasant in Europe and America*, 5 Vols., Chicago, Ill., University of Chicago Press, 1918–1920.

14. MacIver is the author of *Labor in the Changing World*, New York, E. P. Dutton and Co., 1919; *The Modern State*, London, H. Milford, Oxford University Press, 1928; *The Contributions of Sociology to Social Work*,

New York, Columbia University, 1931; *Leviathan and the People*, University Station, Baton Rouge, La., Louisiana State University Press, 1939; *Social Causation*, New York, Ginn & Co., 1942; *Towards an Abiding Peace*, New York, The Macmillan Co., 1943; *The Web of Government*, New York, The Macmillan Co., 1947; *The More Perfect Union*, New York, The Macmillan Co., 1948; *The Ramparts We Guard*, New York, The Macmillan Co., 1950; *Democracy and Economic Challenge*, New York, Alfred A. Knopf, Inc., 1952. He is co-author with Moritz J. Bonn and Ralph Barton Perry of *The Roots of Totalitarianism*, Philadelphia, Pa., The American Academy of Political and Social Science, 1940, and with Charles H. Page of *Society: An Introductory Analysis*, New York, Rhinehart & Co., Inc., 1949. He was editor of *Group Relations and Group Antagonisms*, 1944; *Civilization and Group Relationships*, 1945; *Unity and Difference in American Life*, 1947; *Discrimination and National Welfare*, 1949; *Great Expressions of Human Rights*, 1950; *Conflict of Loyalties*, 1952; all published in New York by Harper & Brothers for the Institute for Religious and Social Studies.

15. Becker's major publications include the following: Wiese-Becker: *Systematic Sociology*, New York, John Wiley & Sons, Inc., 1932; Barnes, Harry Elmer, and Howard Becker: *Social Thought from Lore to Science*, 2 Vols. Boston, D. C. Heath & Co., 1938; Becker, Howard: *German Youth: Bond or Free*, London, K. Paul, Trench, Trubner and Co., Ltd., 1946; Barnes, Harry E., Howard Becker, and Frances B. Becker: *Contemporary Social Theory*, New York, D. Appleton-Century Co., Inc., 1940; (Eds.): Becker, Howard, and Reuben Hill: *Family, Marriage and Parenthood*, Boston, D. C. Heath & Co., 1948; Becker, Howard: *Through Values to Social Interpretation*, Durham, N. C., Duke University Press, 1950.

16. See his *Essays in Sociological Theory*, Glencoe, Ill., The Free Press, 1949.

17. His *The Social System*, Glencoe, Ill., The Free Press, 1951, should be read in conjunction with Parsons, Talcott, and Edward A. Shils (Eds.): *Toward a General Theory of Action*, Cambridge, Mass., Harvard University Press, 1951, and Parsons, Talcott, Robert F. Bales, and Edward A. Shils: *Working Papers in the Theory of Action*, Glencoe, Ill., The Free Press, 1953. These volumes were preceded by Parsons' *The Structure of Social Action* (1937), a second printing of which was issued by The Free Press, 1949.

18. William J. Goode and Paul K. Hatt in *Methods in Social Research*, New York, McGraw-Hill Book Co., Inc., 1952, note on pages 9–16 that theory and fact have reciprocal roles in the scientific method. Their conception of this reciprocity follows Merton's own view in *Social Theory and Social Structure*, Glencoe, Ill., The Free Press, 1949, pp. 83–96 and pp. 97–111.

19. Merton, Robert K.: *Social Theory and Social Structure*, Glencoe, Ill., The Free Press, 1949, pp. 50–54.

20. For illuminating illustrations of this and other functionalist concepts, see Chinoy, Ely: *Sociological Perspective* (Studies in Sociology) New York, Random House, Inc., 1954, pp. 37–47.

21. Merton, *op. cit.* See also Merton, Robert K., Marjorie Fiske, and Alberta Curtis: *Mass Persuasion*, New York, Harper & Brothers, 1946; Merton, Robert K., Marjorie Fiske, and Patricia Kendall: *The Focussed Interview*, 2nd ed. New York, Bureau of Applied Social Research, Columbia University, 1952. Merton is also Editor, with Paul F. Lazarsfeld, of *Continuities in Social Research*, Glencoe, Ill., The Free Press, 1950, and with Ailsa P. Gray, Barbara Hockey, and Hanan C. Selvin of *Reader in Bureaucracy*, Glencoe, Ill., The Free Press, 1952.

chapter four

Retrospect and Prospect

During its first half-century American sociology increasingly diversified its problems of investigation, specialized its methods, and refined its generalizations and theories. These developments were in part a reflection of the process of urbanization and centralization of American society and a response to the critical events of two world wars and a nationwide economic depression. In investigating the problems of the world in which they lived, sociologists utilized prevailing European and American intellectual traditions and resources.

Today American sociology is a firmly established social-scientific discipline possessing its own body of knowledge, concepts, and theories. In contrast to the early years, there are now over four thousand professional sociologists, more and more with urban backgrounds, and employed throughout all regions of the country in all types of academic institutions and in numerous private industries and governmental agencies. So many new sociological periodicals, books, regional and special associations have appeared and the field has become so differentiated and its methods so specialized that the sociology student as a rule finds little time during his professional training to become proficient in other disciplines as well.

While many of the present subfields are outgrowths of the social problems studied during the formative era—for example, criminology, family and marriage, old age, and social and personal disorganization—new specialties have emerged. Some of these new areas, such as communication and public opinion, small-group study, industrial sociology, and social stratification, reflect the new social conditions and relationships of mass society. Other subfields, such as sociology of health, the study of the child, and analyses of authority and leadership, have been more specifically related to the growth of interdisciplinary and large-scale research.

Sociologists have specialized their research techniques without having entirely resolved the older controversy between the quantitative-mathematical and qualitative approaches. Today the initial formulation of the research problem usually specifies the type of procedure to be used, whether attitude scales, questionnaires, and census data or interviews, participant observation, and case-history analysis, or combinations of two or more of these.

As field differentiation and specialization occurred the basic elements of the sociological point of view evidenced some notable modifications and continuities. Since many of these continuities are likely to persist, they embody some clues as to the prospects of the future developments of American sociology.

Sociologists still assume that there is a universal similarity about all human behavior which can eventually be codified as a system of universal interrelated laws. Seeking to construct such a logical system of laws, recent systematic theory differs from earlier endeavors which assumed that investigations of empirical phenomena would reveal laws inherent in nature. Yet the empirical preoccupation so characteristic of the second era of American sociology has not been relinquished entirely. Contemporary sociologists generally follow an approach intermediate to "pure theory" and "raw empiricism" in their quest for the scientific laws of society. It seems likely that at least some of the popularity of Merton's "theories of the middle range" stems from their articulate expression of this scientific approach.

In their efforts to establish laws of human behavior, social structure, and change sociologists use methods patterned after other social and natural sciences, at least implicitly. They tend to emphasize quantification by using measurement and statistical techniques, to approximate experimentation by constructing research designs, and to interrelate their activities by formulating hypotheses drawn from existent principles, generalizations, and laws. Sociologists generally avoid the use of historical materials because historical data are conceived to be essentially unique rather than repetitive and general and consequently unsuitable to measurement or experimentation. Theories of social change are, therefore, often ahistorical and devoid of cultural concreteness.

While sociology is still justified by its usefulness, its direct relationship to humanitarian reformism and meliorism, as based on the rationale of the belief in progress, has been replaced by an explicit or implicit utilitarianism. Nevertheless, there is the implication that such instrumentalism will operate for the common good which, as a consequence of the several national crises, has been equated with national welfare. In order to be useful, sociological research focuses particularly on the goal of prediction and control.

During all three eras of American sociology its individualism, as it has been termed in this study, is perhaps its most significant characteristic. The feeling, knowing, and willing of individuals—though limited by cultural prescriptions and social controls—are taken to be the ultimate source of human interaction, social structure, and social change. A deterministic explanation inimical to this basic postulate of voluntarism finds, and no doubt will find in the future, few protagonists. A sociology of knowledge, for instance, which maintains a strict causal relationship between a specific form of social existence or class position and knowledge is unlikely to gain many adherents among American sociologists. Indeed, most sociological generalizations are specifically formulated as probability statements, thereby reserving a limited amount of freedom for the individual to deviate from the rule or law.

Social behavior is interpreted voluntaristically. Social structures are real only as they are products of individuals in interaction. The social action theory's emphasis on the intentions and goal-orientation of individuals illustrates this viewpoint. Most American sociologists phrase their research

problems from the perspective of individual behavior and generally reinter-
pret more holistic approaches so that they coincide with this individualism.
Consequently, neither Durkheim's notion of society as an entity *sui generis*
nor Marx's interpretation of social stratification in terms of economic relations and consequent class consciousness has been accepted in American
sociology in spite of widespread familiarity with these ideas.

Though influenced by changing American social conditions and crises
and the growth and specialization of the discipline itself, modern American
sociology has thus retained a basic homogeneity of viewpoint. Future developments will probably require investigations into as yet unknown areas
of social life. But judging by the events of the past and current trends,
American sociologists will be likely to explain such behavior, social organization, and change by universal laws based on the motivation of individuals in interaction.

Selected Readings

Barnes, Harry Elmer: *An Introduction to the History of Sociology*, Chicago, University
of Chicago Press, 1948.
     Contains detailed analyses of major American and European sociologists. See espe-
cially the selections on Comte, Spencer, Sumner, Ward, Ross, Giddings, Small,
Cooley, Ellwood, Thomas, Durkheim, and Weber.

Barnes, Harry E., Howard Becker, and Frances B. Becker (Eds.): *Contemporary Social
Theory*, New York, D. Appleton-Century Co., Inc., 1940.
     A symposium discussing recent methodological problems, the contributions of other
sciences to sociology, and the application of sociological theory.

Beal, Owen F.: *The Development of Sociology in the United States*, Ann Arbor, Mich.,
Edwards Brothers, Inc., 1944.
     A brief but lucid and informative presentation of the contributions of Ward, Sumner,
Small, and Giddings.

Bernard, L. L., and Jessie Bernard: *Origins of American Sociology*, New York, Thomas Y.
Crowell Co., 1943.
     A detailed historical study of the nineteenth-century social and intellectual back-
grounds of American sociology.

Gurvitch, Georges and Wilbert E. Moore: *Twentieth Century Sociology*, New York,
Philosophical Library, Inc., 1945.
     Treats recent viewpoints, methods, and subfields of American sociology and sum-
marizes the state of sociology in selected foreign countries.

Hofstadter, Richard: *Social Darwinism in American Thought*, Philadelphia, University of
Pennsylvania Press, 1945.
     A social-historical statement of nineteenth-century evolutionary theories of change,
emphasizing their sociointellectual context.

House, Floyd N.: *The Development of Sociology*, New York, McGraw-Hill Book Co., Inc.,
1936.
     A general history of social thought with special emphasis on earlier phases of Amer-
ican sociology.

Odum, Howard W.: *American Sociology*, New York, Longmans, Green and Co., Inc.,
1951.
     Discusses the history of American sociology by means of biographical sketches of the
presidents of the American Sociological Society and descriptions of developments in
major fields.

Shils, Edward: *The Present State of American Sociology*, Glencoe, Ill., The Free Press,
1948.
     A brief, readable commentary on the nature, changes, and literature of recent Amer-
ican sociology.